R.I.P.D.™

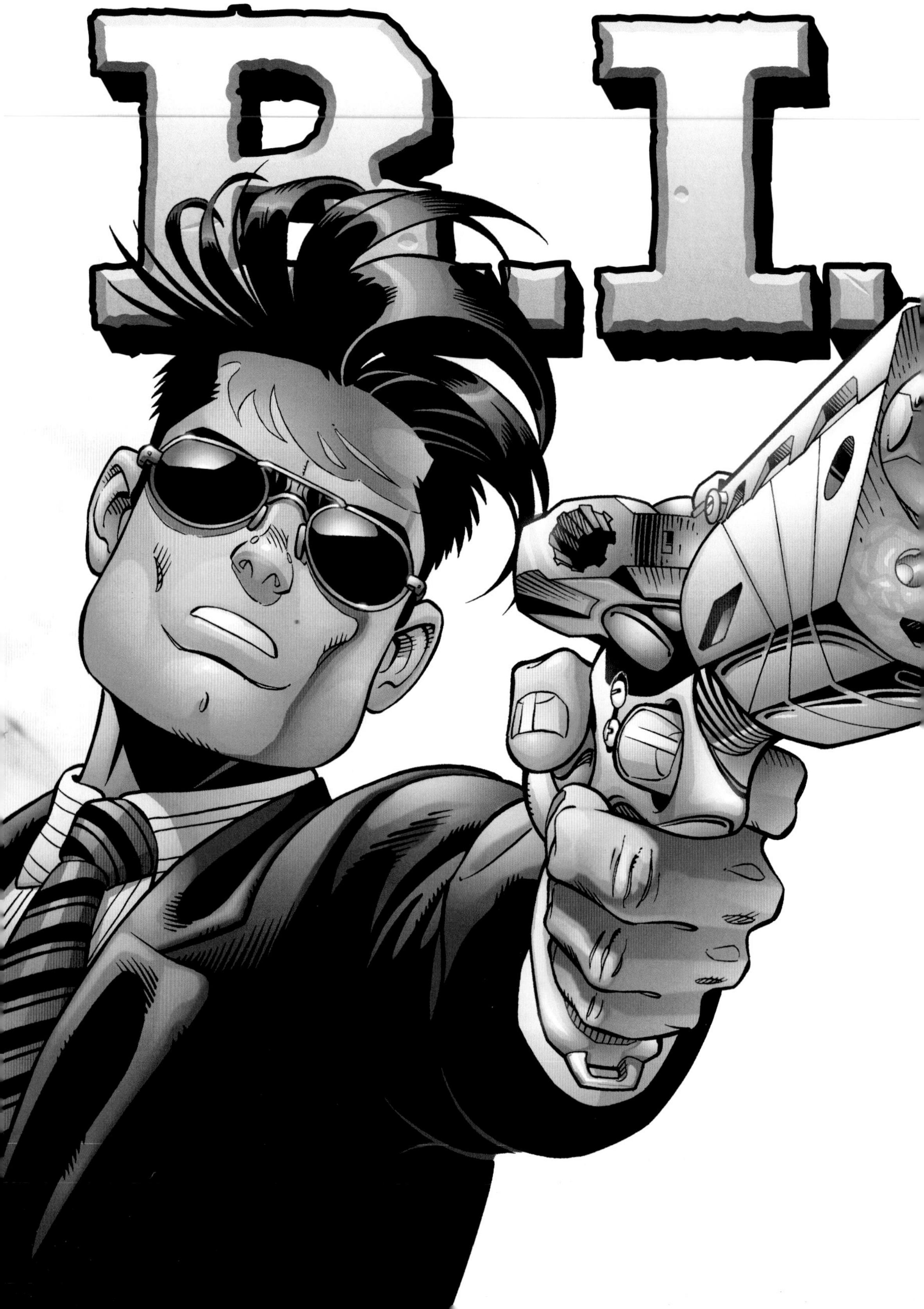
P.I.

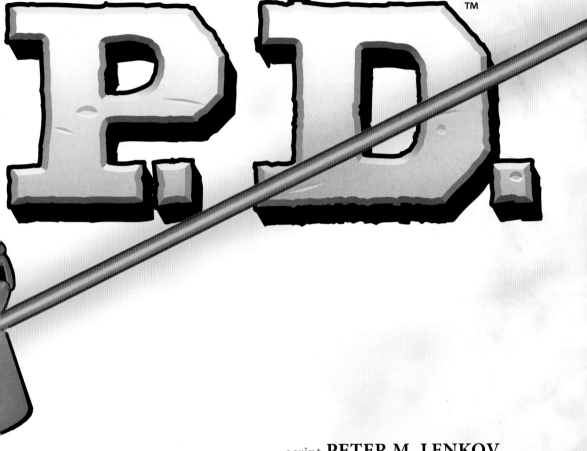

script **PETER M. LENKOV**

pencils **LUCAS MARANGON**

inks **RANDY EMBERLIN**

colors **DAVE NESTELLE**

letters **STEVE DUTRO**

cover **DAVE WILKINS**

 DARK HORSE BOOKS

Publisher **Mike Richardson**

Original Series Editor **Dave Land**

Original Series Assistant Editor **Philip Simon**

Collection Editor **Patrick Thorpe**

Collection Designer **Tina Alessi**

Digital Art and Production **Christianne Goudreau**

This volume collects issues #1–#4 of Dark Horse Comics' series *R.I.P.D.*, first published in 1999 and 2000.

Check out *R.I.P.D.: City of the Damned*, a new miniseries by Jeremy Barlow and Tony Parker, from Dark Horse Comics.

Published by
Dark Horse Books
A division of Dark Horse Comics, Inc.
10956 SE Main Street
Milwaukie, OR 97222

DarkHorse.com

To find a comics shop in your area, call the Comic Shop
Locator Service toll-free at 1-888-266-4226.

Second edition: March 2013
ISBN 978-1-61655-071-4
10 9 8 7 6 5 4 3 2 1
Printed in China

MIKE RICHARDSON President and Publisher NEIL HANKERSON Executive Vice President TOM WEDDLE Chief Financial Officer RANDY STRADLEY Vice President of Publishing MICHAEL MARTENS Vice President of Book Trade Sales ANITA NELSON Vice President of Business Affairs SCOTT ALLIE Editor in Chief MATT PARKINSON Vice President of Marketing DAVID SCROGGY Vice President of Product Development DALE LAFOUNTAIN Vice President of Information Technology DARLENE VOGEL Senior Director of Print, Design, and Production KEN LIZZI General Counsel DAVEY ESTRADA Editorial Director CHRIS WARNER Senior Books Editor DIANA SCHUTZ Executive Editor CARY GRAZZINI Director of Print and Development LIA RIBACCHI Art Director CARA NIECE Director of Scheduling TIM WIESCH Director of International Licensing MARK BERNARDI Director of Digital Publishing

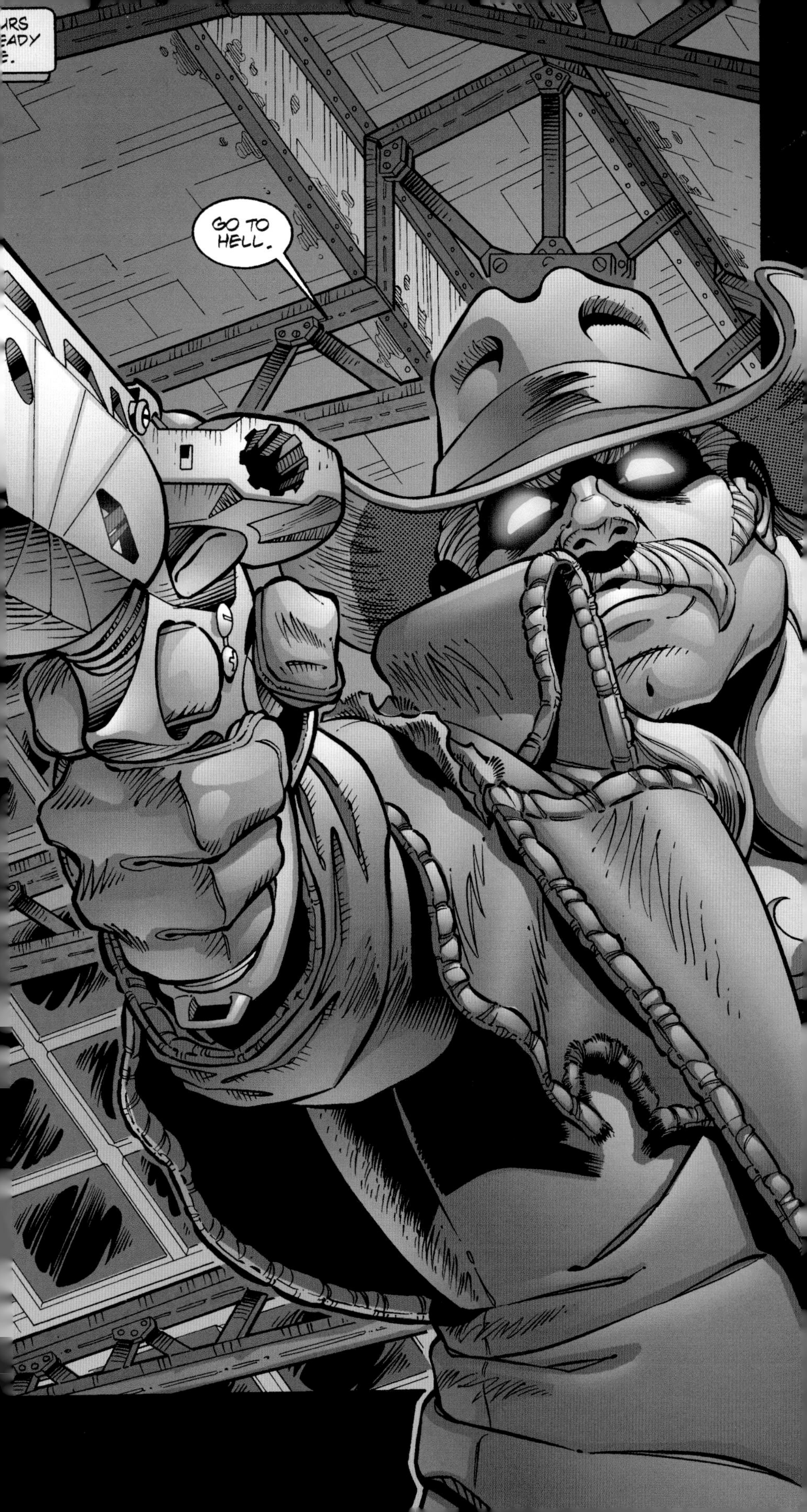
GO TO HELL.

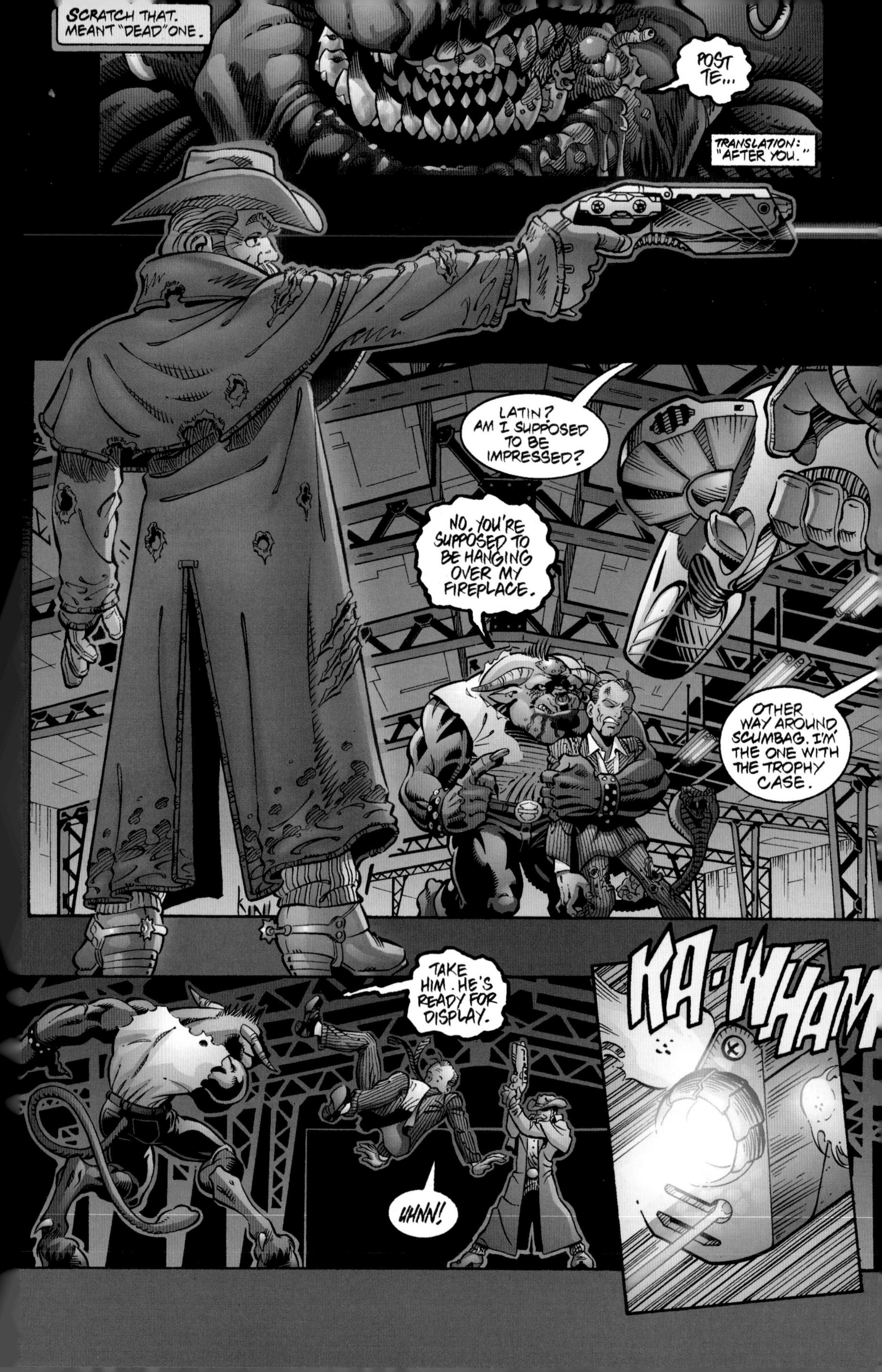
SCRATCH THAT. MEANT "DEAD" ONE.
POST TE...
TRANSLATION: "AFTER YOU."
LATIN? AM I SUPPOSED TO BE IMPRESSED?
NO. YOU'RE SUPPOSED TO BE HANGING OVER MY FIREPLACE.
OTHER WAY AROUND SCUMBAG. I'M THE ONE WITH THE TROPHY CASE.
TAKE HIM. HE'S READY FOR DISPLAY.
UHNN!
KA-WHAM

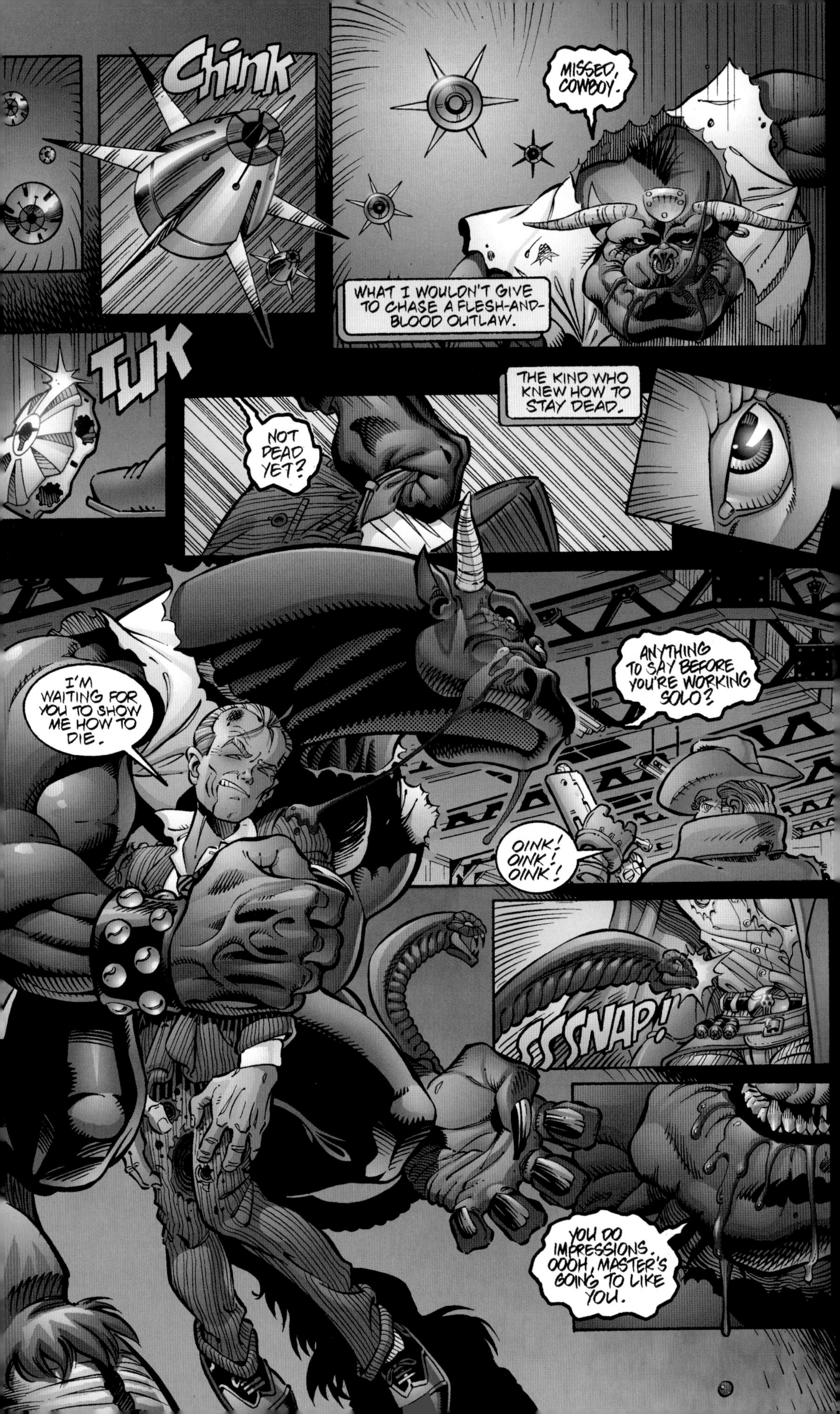
CHINK
MISSED, COWBOY.
WHAT I WOULDN'T GIVE TO CHASE A FLESH-AND-BLOOD OUTLAW.
TUK
THE KIND WHO KNEW HOW TO STAY DEAD.
NOT DEAD YET?
I'M WAITING FOR YOU TO SHOW ME HOW TO DIE.
ANYTHING TO SAY BEFORE YOU'RE WORKING SOLO?
OINK! OINK! OINK!
SSSNAP!
YOU DO IMPRESSIONS. OOOH, MASTER'S GOING TO LIKE YOU.

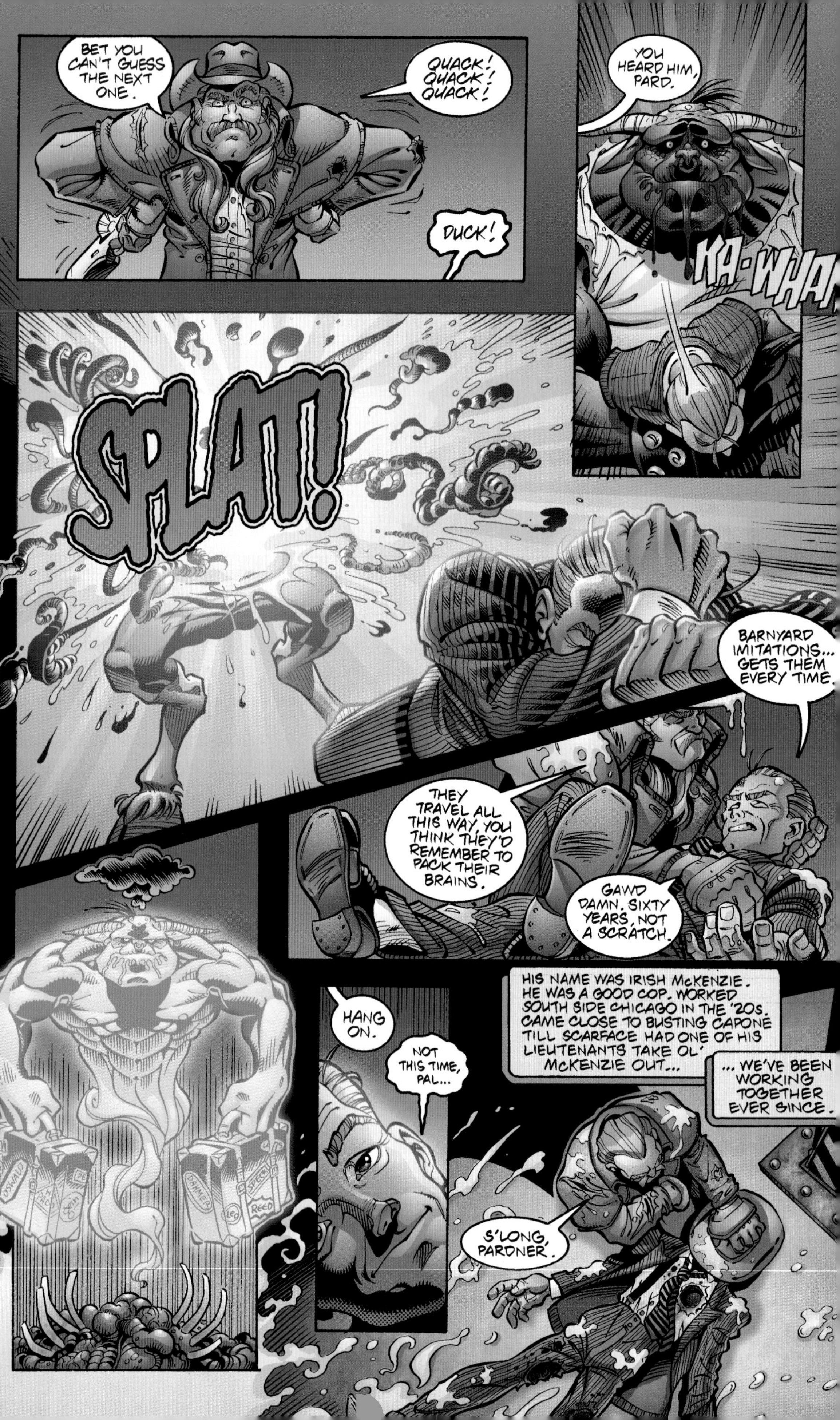

BET YOU CAN'T GUESS THE NEXT ONE.
QUACK! QUACK! QUACK!
DUCK!
YOU HEARD HIM, PARD.
KA-WHA
SPLAT!
BARNYARD IMITATIONS... GETS THEM EVERY TIME.
THEY TRAVEL ALL THIS WAY, YOU THINK THEY'D REMEMBER TO PACK THEIR BRAINS.
GAWD DAMN. SIXTY YEARS, NOT A SCRATCH.
OSWALD
DAHMER
SPECK
REED
HANG ON.
NOT THIS TIME, PAL...
HIS NAME WAS IRISH McKENZIE. HE WAS A GOOD COP. WORKED SOUTH SIDE CHICAGO IN THE '20s. CAME CLOSE TO BUSTING CAPONE TILL SCARFACE HAD ONE OF HIS LIEUTENANTS TAKE OL' McKENZIE OUT...
... WE'VE BEEN WORKING TOGETHER EVER SINCE.
S'LONG, PARDNER.

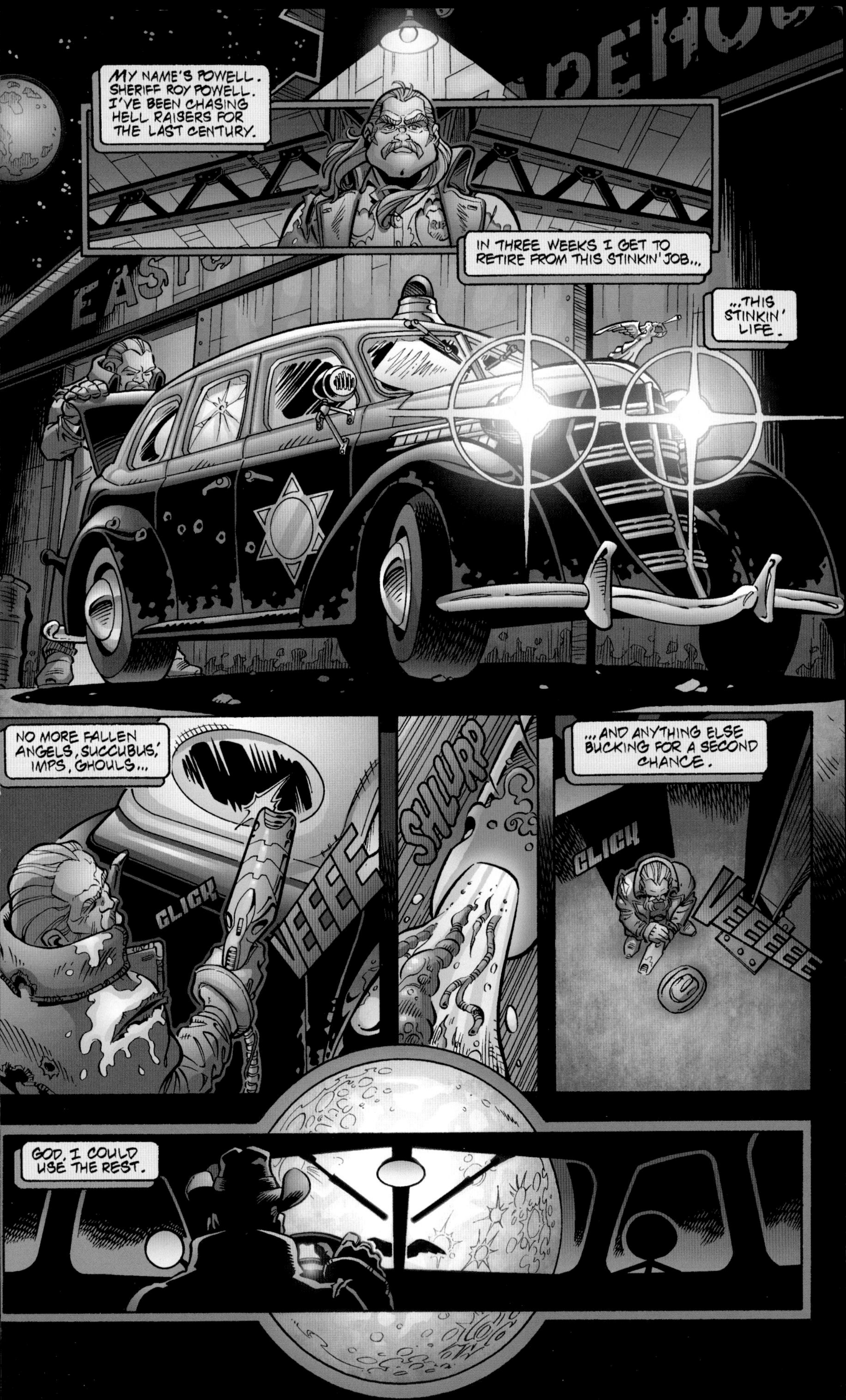

MY NAME'S POWELL. SHERIFF ROY POWELL. I'VE BEEN CHASING HELL RAISERS FOR THE LAST CENTURY.
IN THREE WEEKS I GET TO RETIRE FROM THIS STINKIN' JOB...
...THIS STINKIN' LIFE.
NO MORE FALLEN ANGELS, SUCCUBUS,' IMPS, GHOULS...
CLICK
VEEEE
SHLURP
...AND ANYTHING ELSE BUCKING FOR A SECOND CHANCE.
CLICK
VEEEEE
GOD, I COULD USE THE REST.

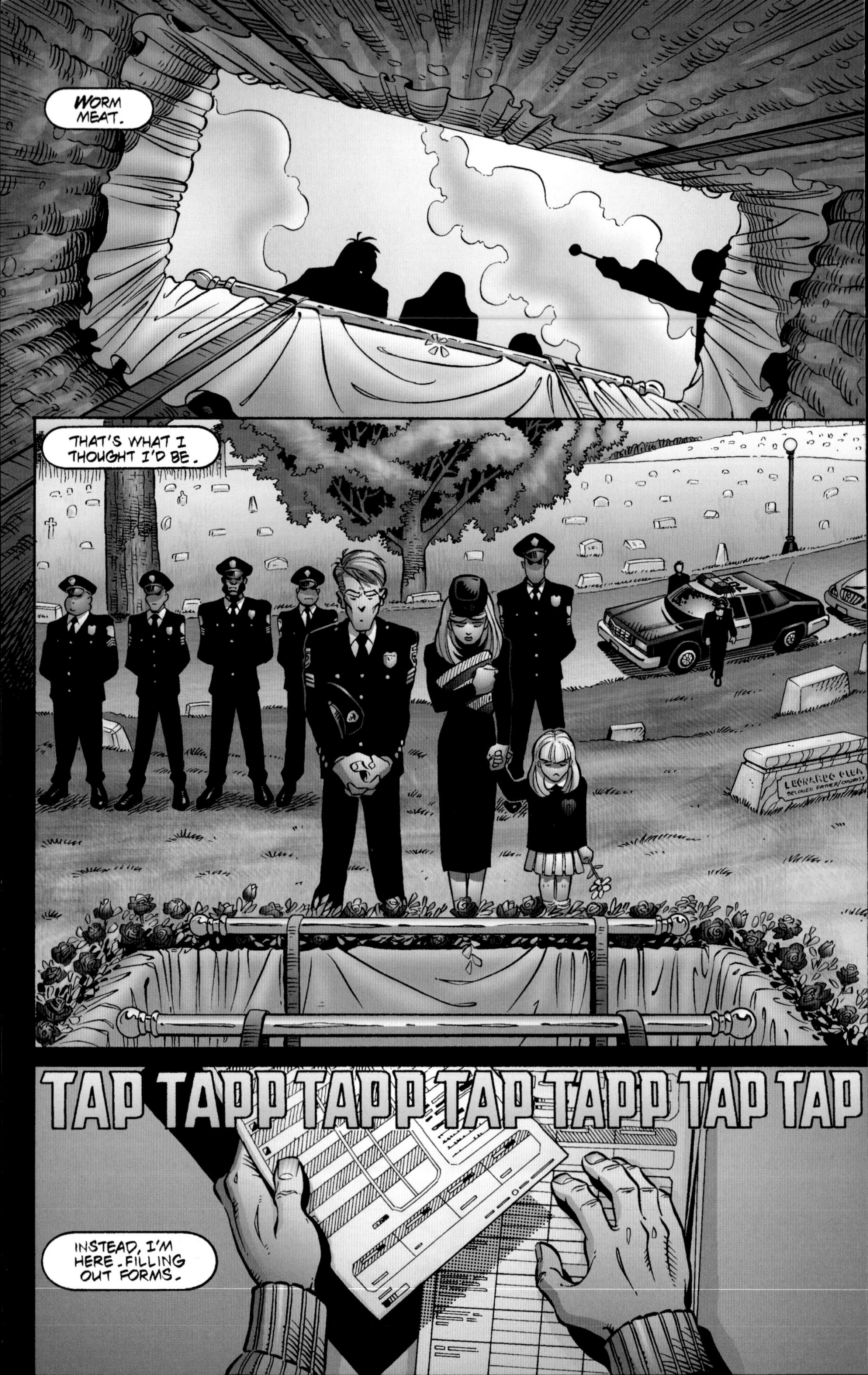
WORM MEAT.
THAT'S WHAT I THOUGHT I'D BE.
BELOVED FATHER/COLORIST
TAP TAPP TAPP TAP TAPP TAP TAP
INSTEAD, I'M HERE. FILLING OUT FORMS.

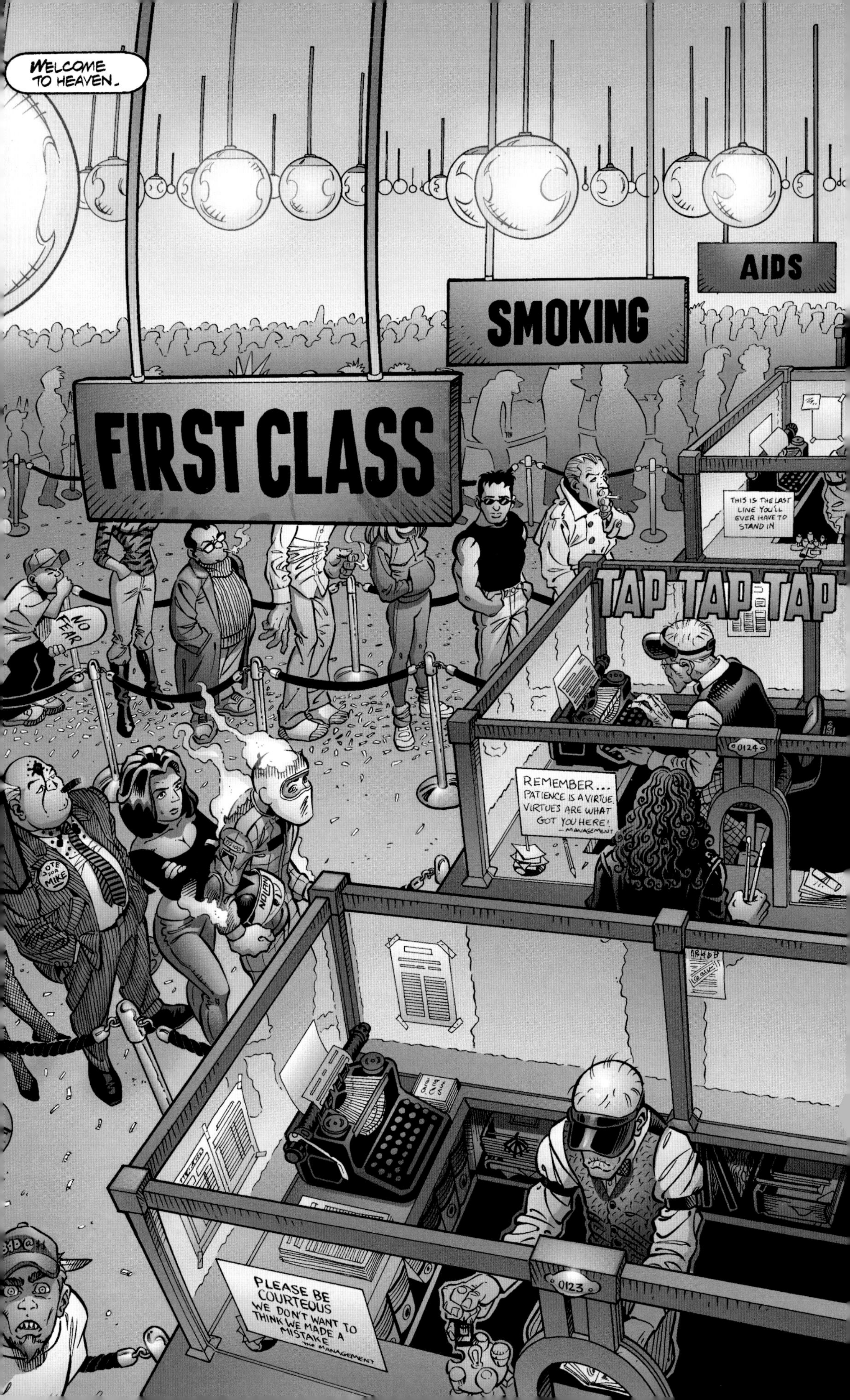
WELCOME TO HEAVEN.
AIDS
SMOKING
FIRST CLASS
THIS IS THE LAST LINE YOU'LL EVER HAVE TO STAND IN
NO FEAR
TAP TAP TAP
0124
REMEMBER... PATIENCE IS A VIRTUE. VIRTUES ARE WHAT GOT YOU HERE! —MANAGEMENT
VOTE FOR MIKE
PLEASE BE COURTEOUS WE DON'T WANT TO THINK WE MADE A MISTAKE THE MANAGEMENT
0123

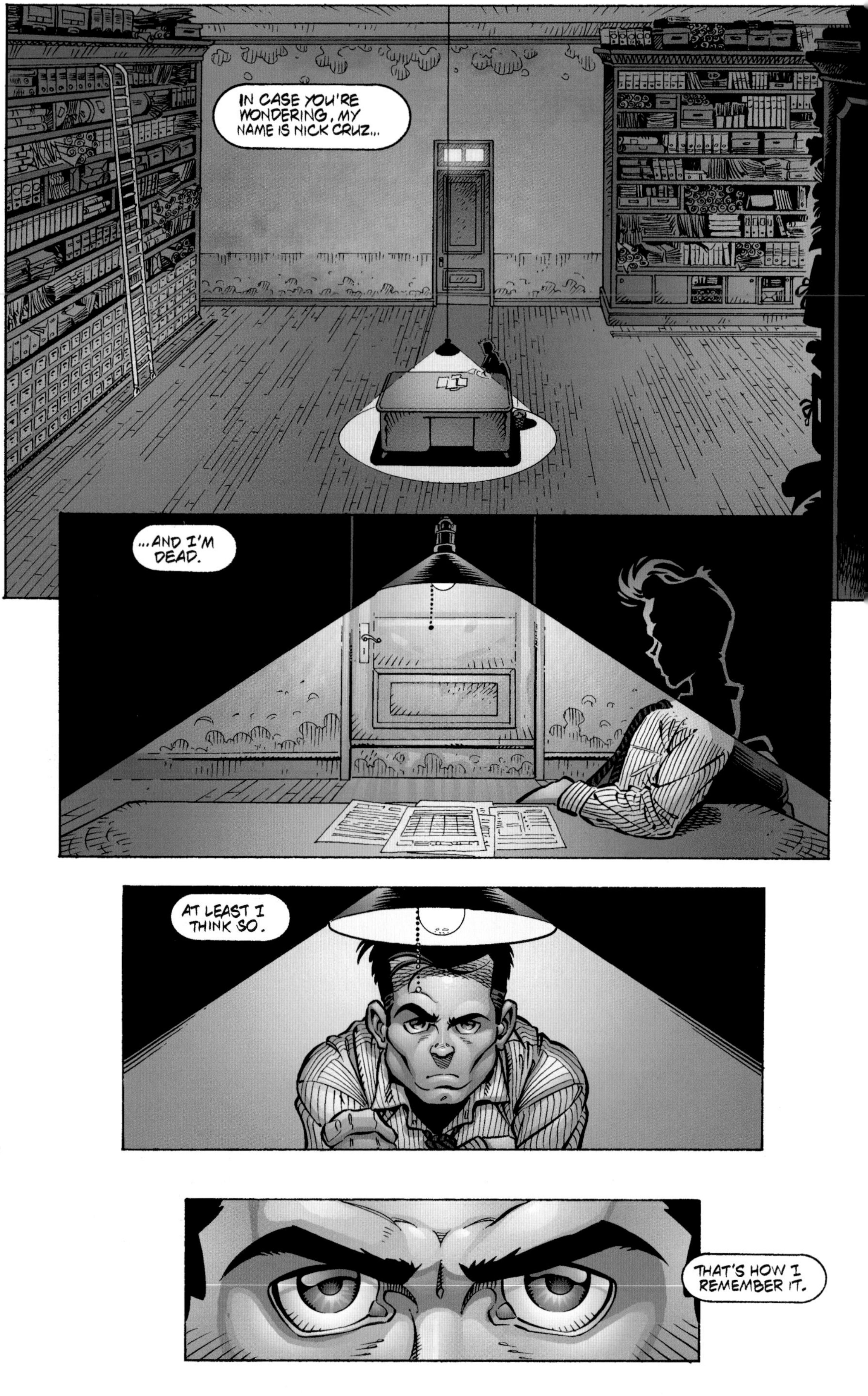
IN CASE YOU'RE WONDERING, MY NAME IS NICK CRUZ...
...AND I'M DEAD.
AT LEAST I THINK SO.
THAT'S HOW I REMEMBER IT.

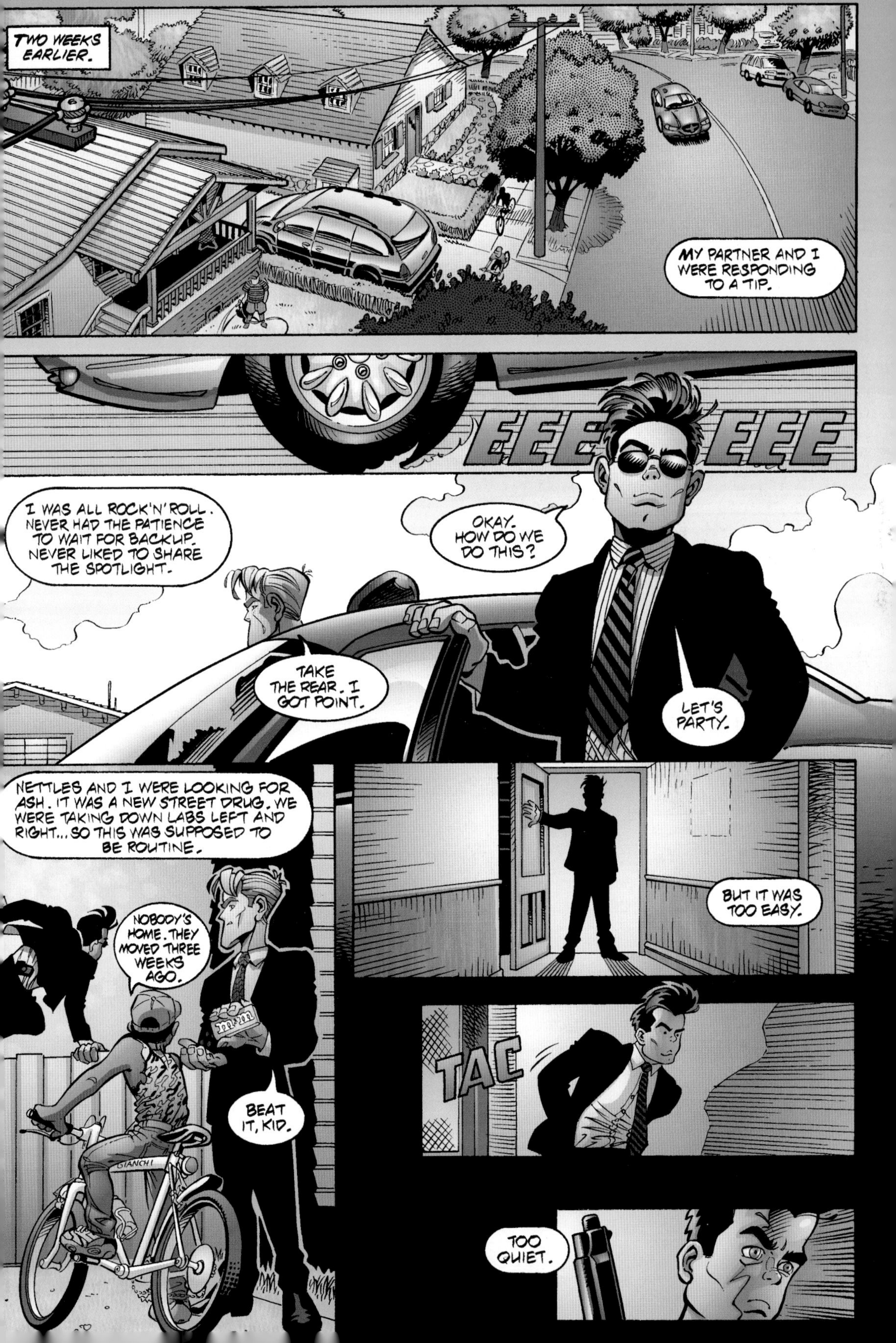

TWO WEEKS EARLIER.
MY PARTNER AND I WERE RESPONDING TO A TIP.
EEE EEE
I WAS ALL ROCK'N'ROLL. NEVER HAD THE PATIENCE TO WAIT FOR BACKUP. NEVER LIKED TO SHARE THE SPOTLIGHT.
OKAY. HOW DO WE DO THIS?
TAKE THE REAR. I GOT POINT.
LET'S PARTY.
NETTLES AND I WERE LOOKING FOR ASH. IT WAS A NEW STREET DRUG. WE WERE TAKING DOWN LABS LEFT AND RIGHT... SO THIS WAS SUPPOSED TO BE ROUTINE.
NOBODY'S HOME. THEY MOVED THREE WEEKS AGO.
BEAT IT, KID.
GIANCHI
BUT IT WAS TOO EASY.
TAC
TOO QUIET.

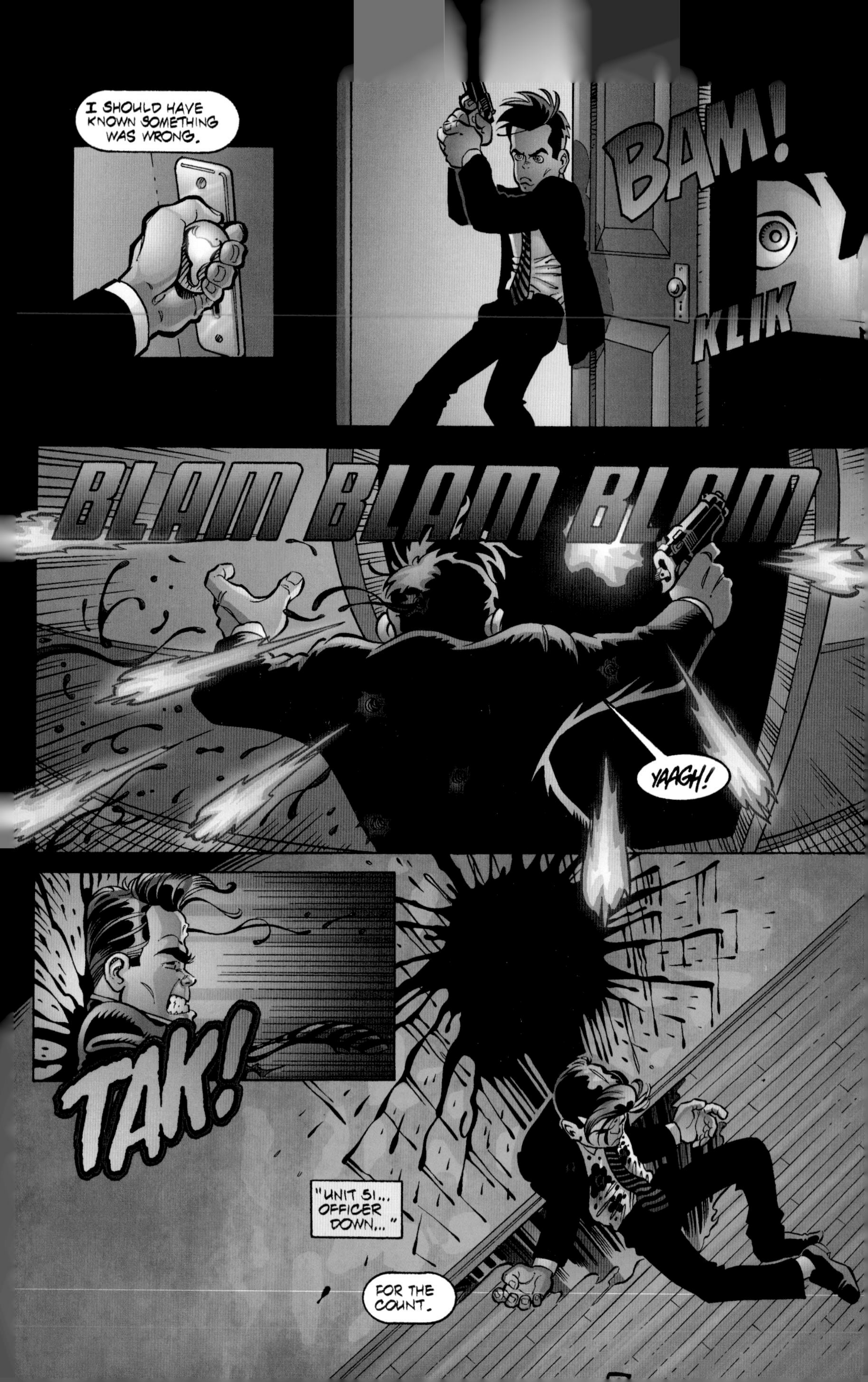
I SHOULD HAVE KNOWN SOMETHING WAS WRONG.
BAM!
KLIK
BLAM BLAM BLAM
YAAGH!
TAK!
"UNIT 51... OFFICER DOWN..."
FOR THE COUNT.

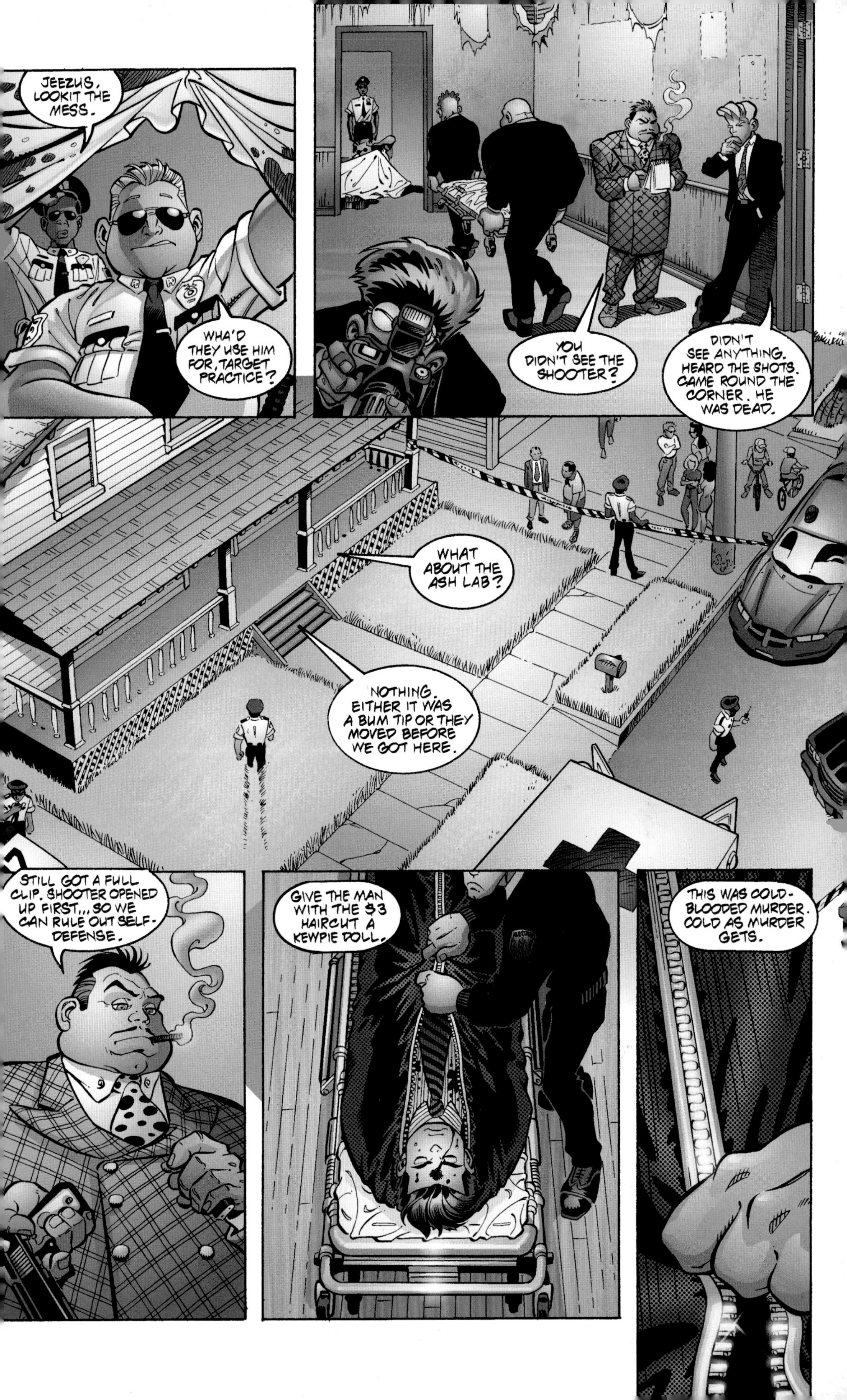
JEEZUS, LOOKIT THE MESS.
WHA'D THEY USE HIM FOR, TARGET PRACTICE?
YOU DIDN'T SEE THE SHOOTER?
DIDN'T SEE ANYTHING. HEARD THE SHOTS. CAME ROUND THE CORNER. HE WAS DEAD.
WHAT ABOUT THE ASH LAB?
NOTHING. EITHER IT WAS A BUM TIP OR THEY MOVED BEFORE WE GOT HERE.
STILL GOT A FULL CLIP. SHOOTER OPENED UP FIRST... SO WE CAN RULE OUT SELF-DEFENSE.
GIVE THE MAN WITH THE $3 HAIRCUT A KEWPIE DOLL.
THIS WAS COLD-BLOODED MURDER. COLD AS MURDER GETS.

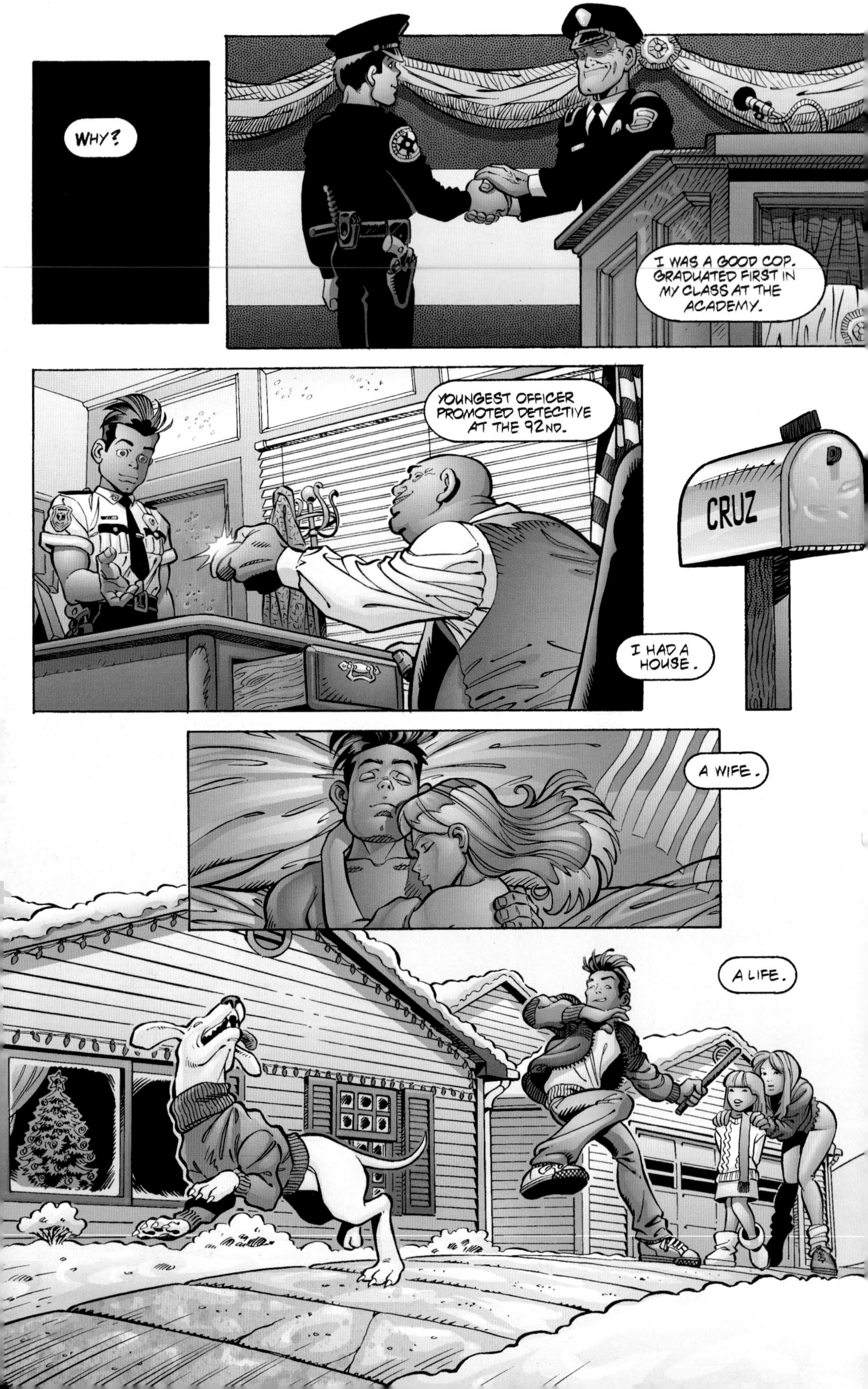
WHY?
I WAS A GOOD COP. GRADUATED FIRST IN MY CLASS AT THE ACADEMY.
YOUNGEST OFFICER PROMOTED DETECTIVE AT THE 92ND.
CRUZ
I HAD A HOUSE.
A WIFE.
A LIFE.

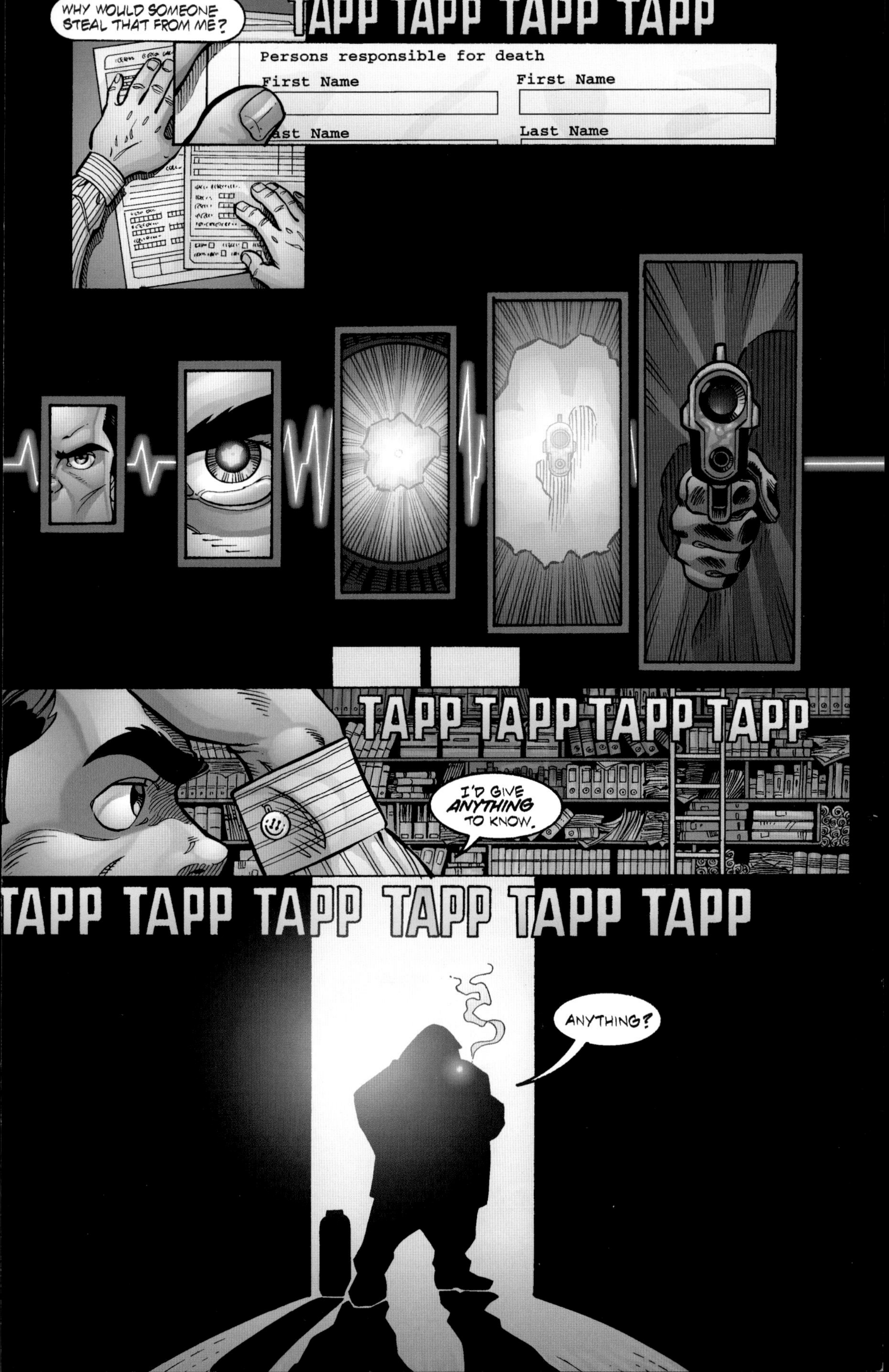
WHY WOULD SOMEONE STEAL THAT FROM ME?
TAPP TAPP TAPP TAPP
Persons responsible for death
First Name
First Name
Last Name
Last Name
TAPP TAPP TAPP TAPP
I'D GIVE ANYTHING TO KNOW.
TAPP TAPP TAPP TAPP TAPP TAPP
ANYTHING?

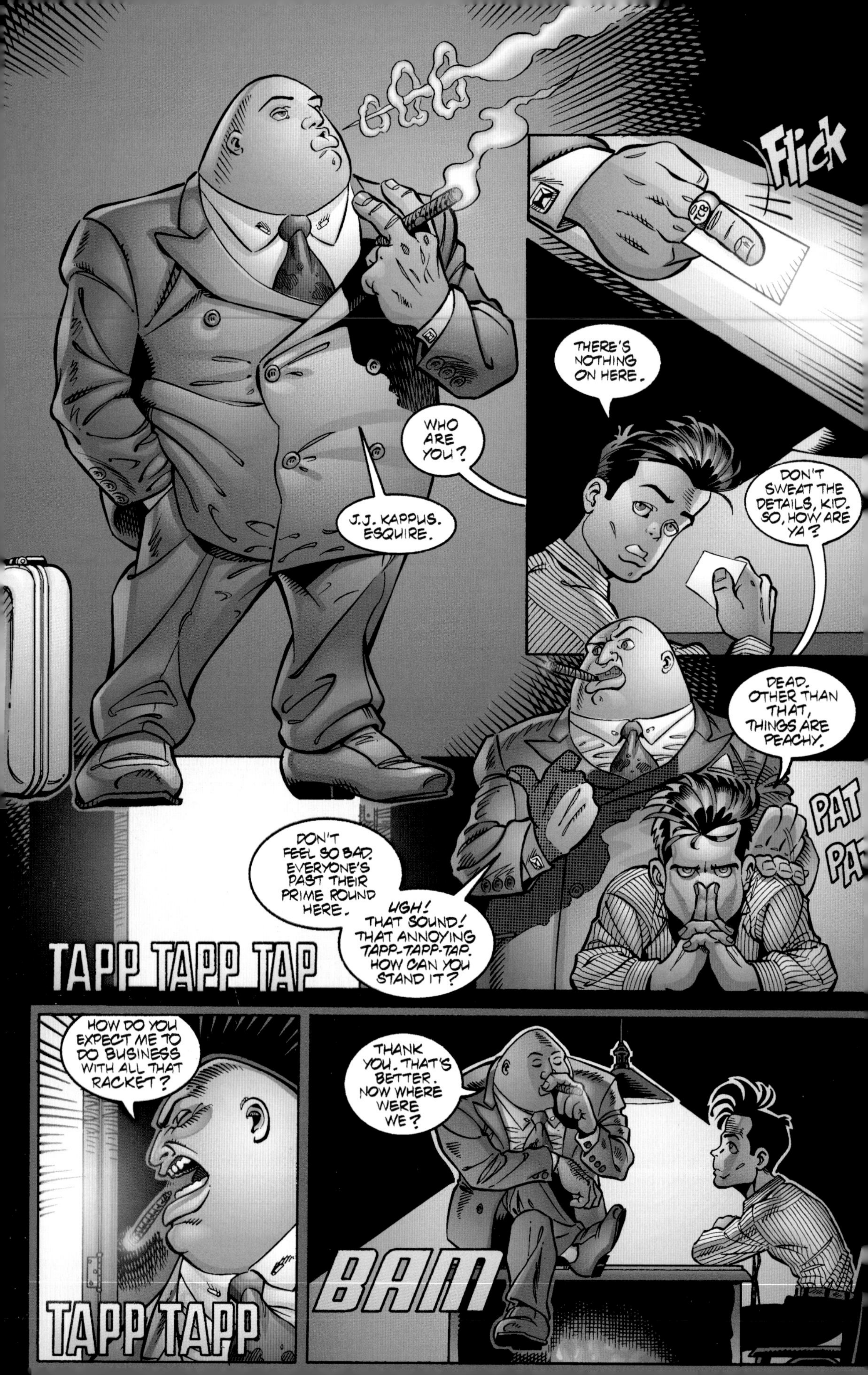
FLICK
THERE'S NOTHING ON HERE.
WHO ARE YOU?
J.J. KAPPUS. ESQUIRE.
DON'T SWEAT THE DETAILS, KID. SO, HOW ARE YA?
DEAD. OTHER THAN THAT, THINGS ARE PEACHY.
PAT
DON'T FEEL SO BAD. EVERYONE'S PAST THEIR PRIME ROUND HERE.
UGH! THAT SOUND! THAT ANNOYING TAPP-TAPP-TAP. HOW CAN YOU STAND IT?
TAPP TAPP TAP
HOW DO YOU EXPECT ME TO DO BUSINESS WITH ALL THAT RACKET?
TAPP TAPP
THANK YOU. THAT'S BETTER. NOW WHERE WERE WE?
BAM

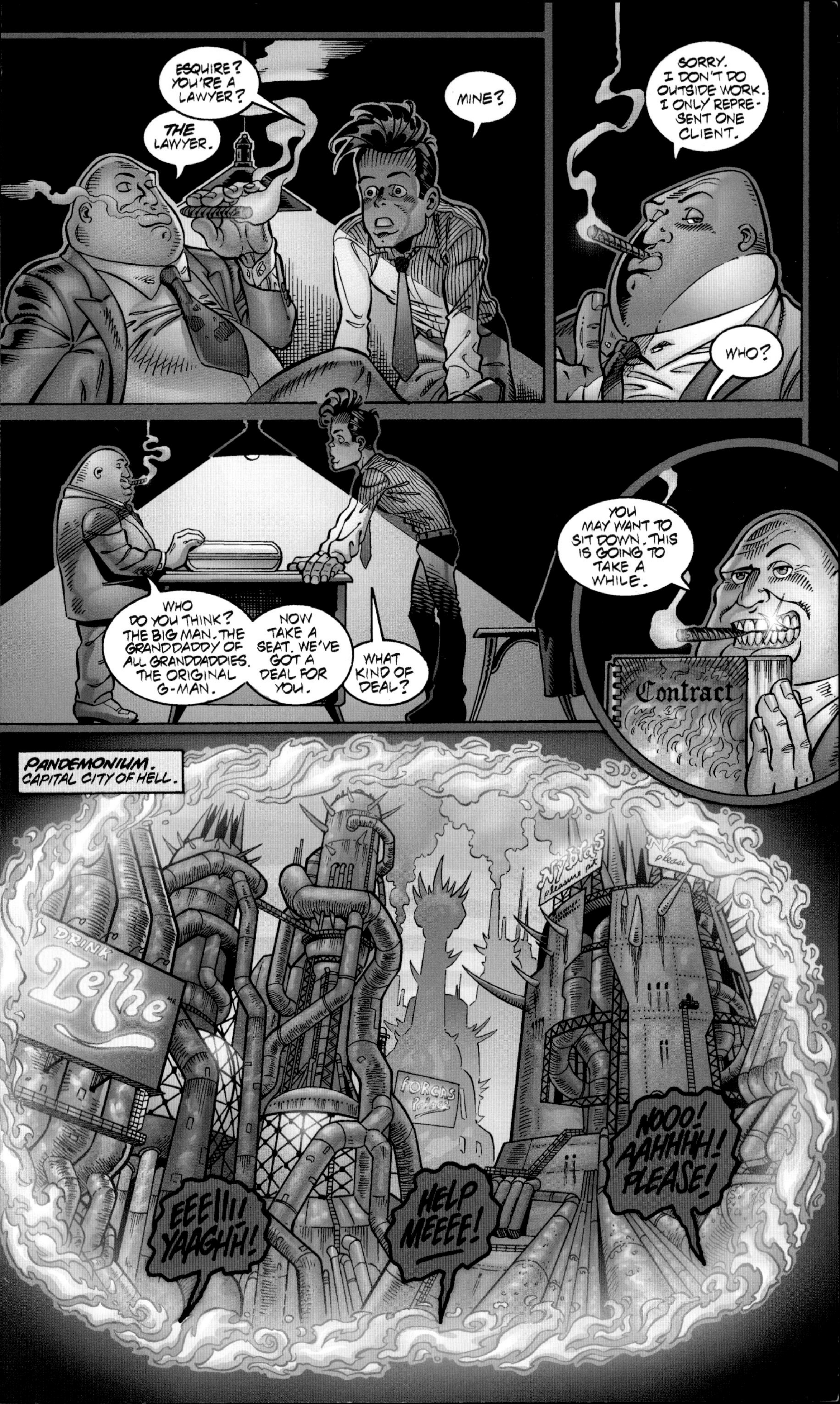
ESQUIRE? YOU'RE A LAWYER?
THE LAWYER.
MINE?
SORRY. I DON'T DO OUTSIDE WORK. I ONLY REPRESENT ONE CLIENT.
WHO?
WHO DO YOU THINK? THE BIG MAN. THE GRANDDADDY OF ALL GRANDDADDIES. THE ORIGINAL G-MAN.
NOW TAKE A SEAT. WE'VE GOT A DEAL FOR YOU.
WHAT KIND OF DEAL?
YOU MAY WANT TO SIT DOWN. THIS IS GOING TO TAKE A WHILE.
Contract
PANDEMONIUM. CAPITAL CITY OF HELL.
DRINK Lethe
FORCAS Palace
EEE!!!! YAAGHH!
HELP MEEEE!
NOOO! AAHHHH! PLEASE!

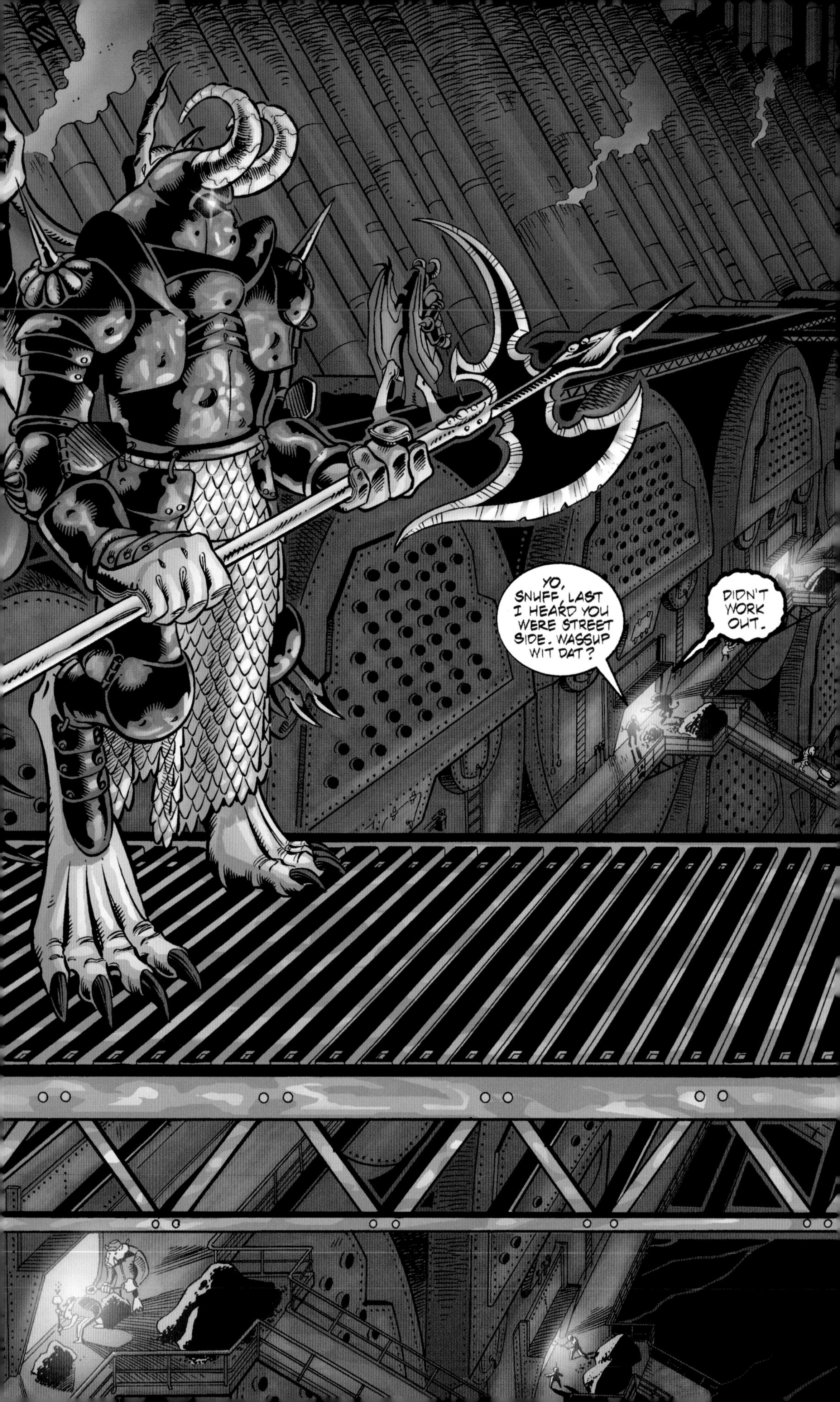
YO, SNUFF, LAST I HEARD YOU WERE STREET SIDE. WASSUP WIT DAT?
DIDN'T WORK OUT.

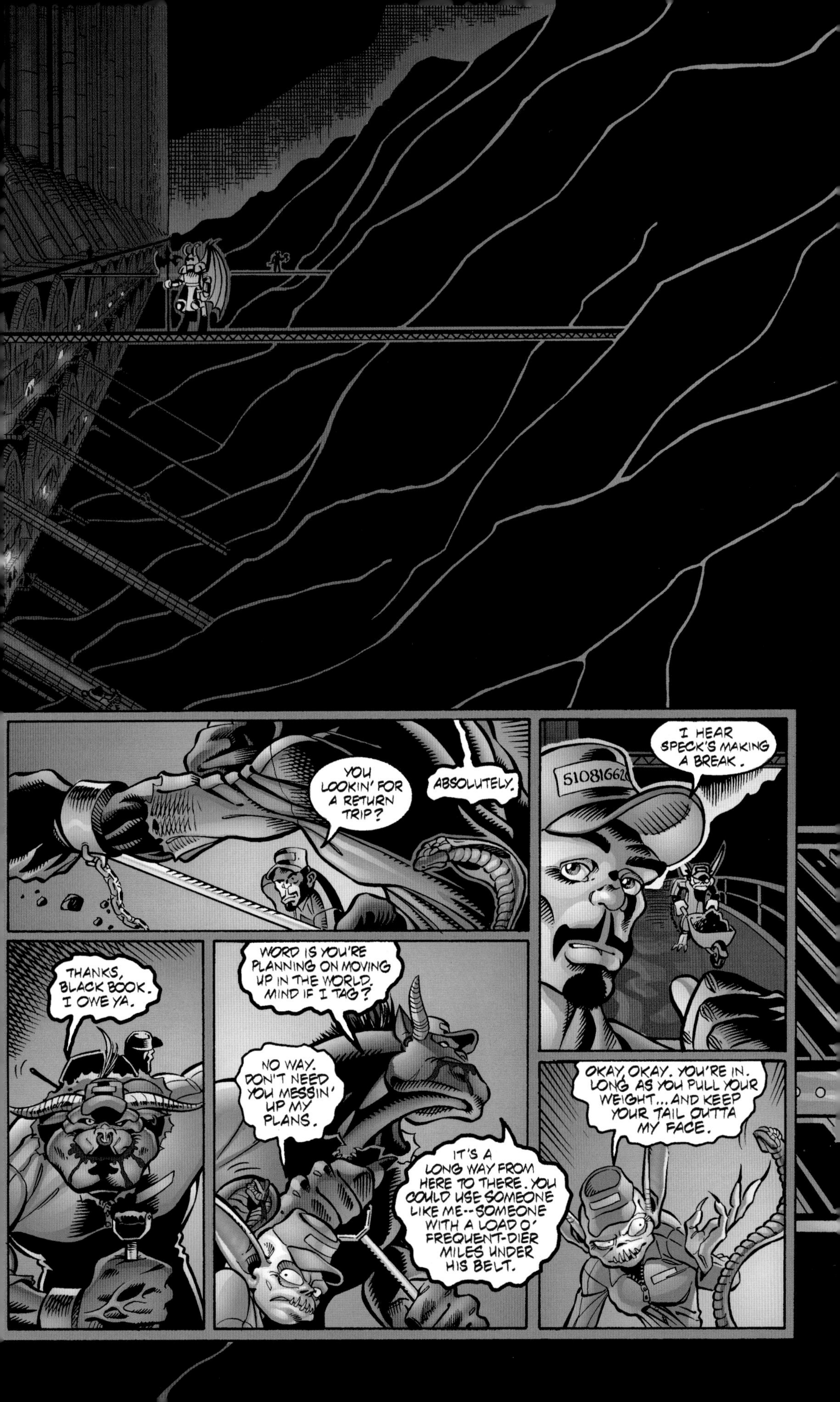

YOU LOOKIN' FOR A RETURN TRIP?
ABSOLUTELY.
I HEAR SPECK'S MAKING A BREAK.
510816626
THANKS, BLACK BOOK. I OWE YA.
WORD IS YOU'RE PLANNING ON MOVING UP IN THE WORLD. MIND IF I TAG?
NO WAY. DON'T NEED YOU MESSIN' UP MY PLANS.
IT'S A LONG WAY FROM HERE TO THERE. YOU COULD USE SOMEONE LIKE ME--SOMEONE WITH A LOAD O' FREQUENT-DIER MILES UNDER HIS BELT.
OKAY, OKAY. YOU'RE IN. LONG AS YOU PULL YOUR WEIGHT... AND KEEP YOUR TAIL OUTTA MY FACE.

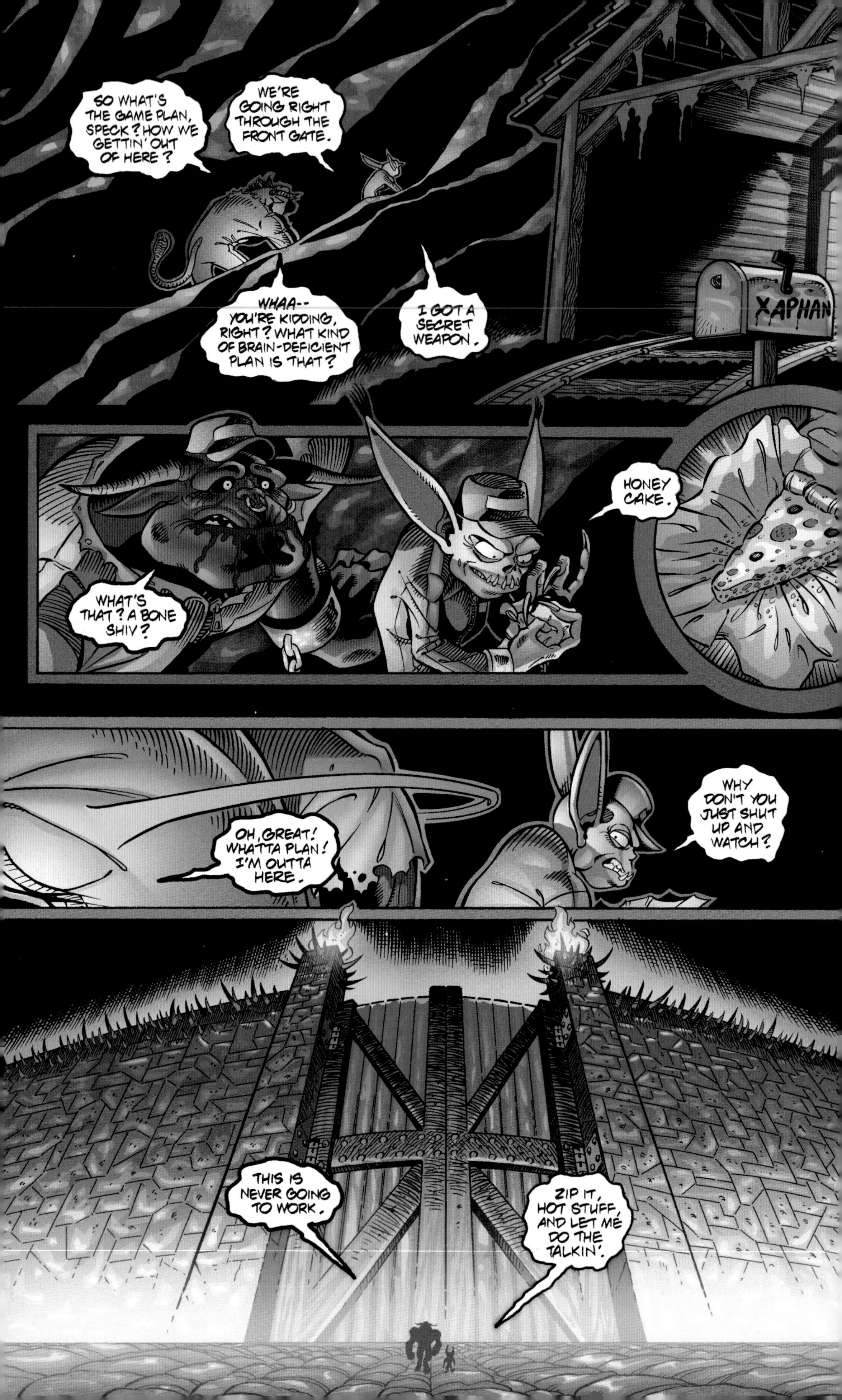
SO WHAT'S THE GAME PLAN, SPECK? HOW WE GETTIN' OUT OF HERE?
WE'RE GOING RIGHT THROUGH THE FRONT GATE.
WHAA-- YOU'RE KIDDING, RIGHT? WHAT KIND OF BRAIN-DEFICIENT PLAN IS THAT?
I GOT A SECRET WEAPON.
XAPHAN
WHAT'S THAT? A BONE SHIV?
HONEY CAKE.
OH, GREAT! WHATTA PLAN! I'M OUTTA HERE.
WHY DON'T YOU JUST SHUT UP AND WATCH?
THIS IS NEVER GOING TO WORK.
ZIP IT, HOT STUFF, AND LET ME DO THE TALKIN'.

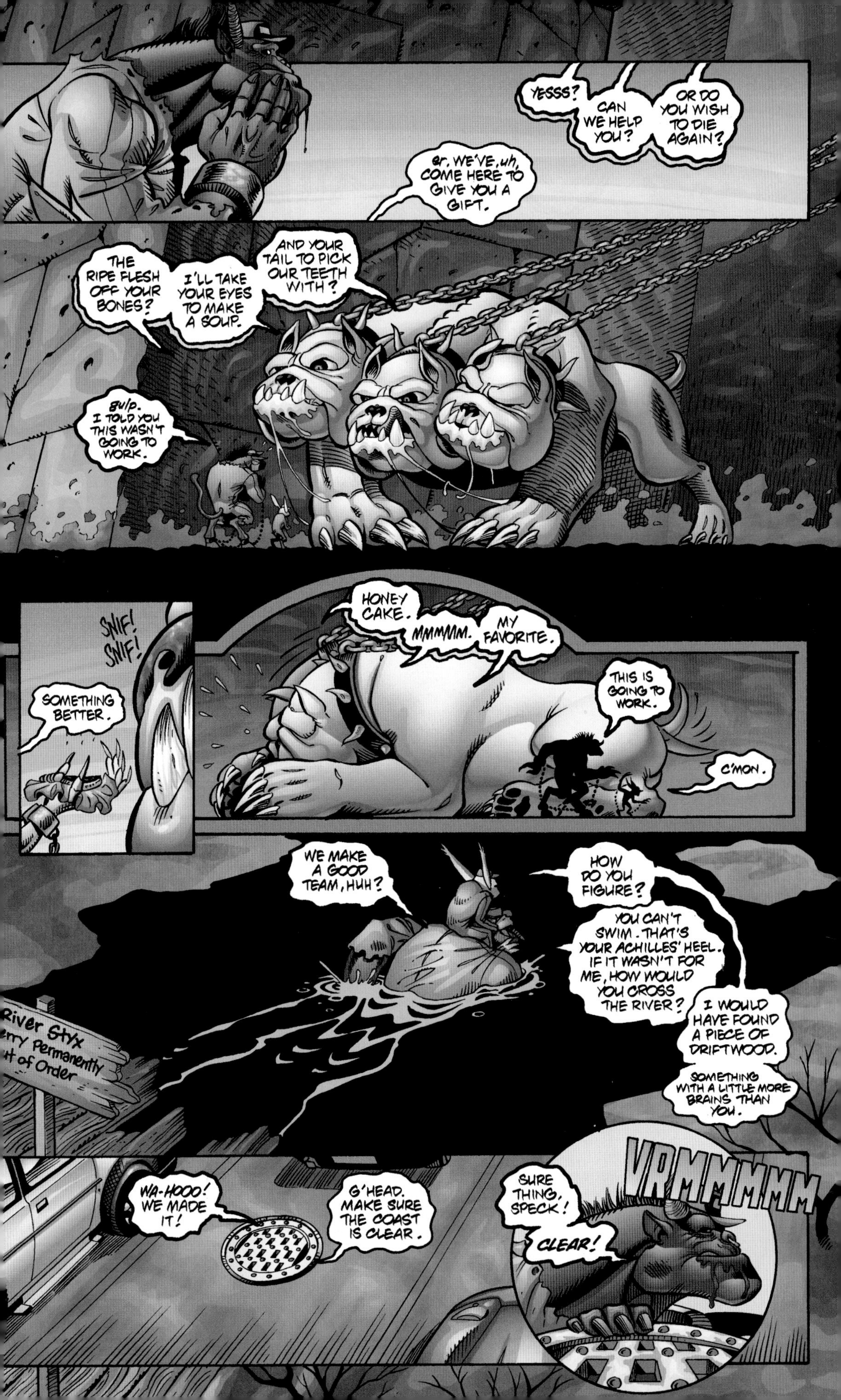
YESSS?
CAN WE HELP YOU?
OR DO YOU WISH TO DIE AGAIN?
er, WE'VE, uh, COME HERE TO GIVE YOU A GIFT.
THE RIPE FLESH OFF YOUR BONES?
I'LL TAKE YOUR EYES TO MAKE A SOUP.
AND YOUR TAIL TO PICK OUR TEETH WITH?
gulp. I TOLD YOU THIS WASN'T GOING TO WORK.
SNIF! SNIF!
SOMETHING BETTER.
HONEY CAKE.
MMMMM.
MY FAVORITE.
THIS IS GOING TO WORK.
C'MON.
WE MAKE A GOOD TEAM, HUH?
HOW DO YOU FIGURE?
YOU CAN'T SWIM. THAT'S YOUR ACHILLES' HEEL. IF IT WASN'T FOR ME, HOW WOULD YOU CROSS THE RIVER?
I WOULD HAVE FOUND A PIECE OF DRIFTWOOD.
SOMETHING WITH A LITTLE MORE BRAINS THAN YOU.
River Styx
erry Permanently
ut of Order
WA-HOOO! WE MADE IT!
G'HEAD. MAKE SURE THE COAST IS CLEAR.
SURE THING, SPECK!
CLEAR!
VRMMMMMM

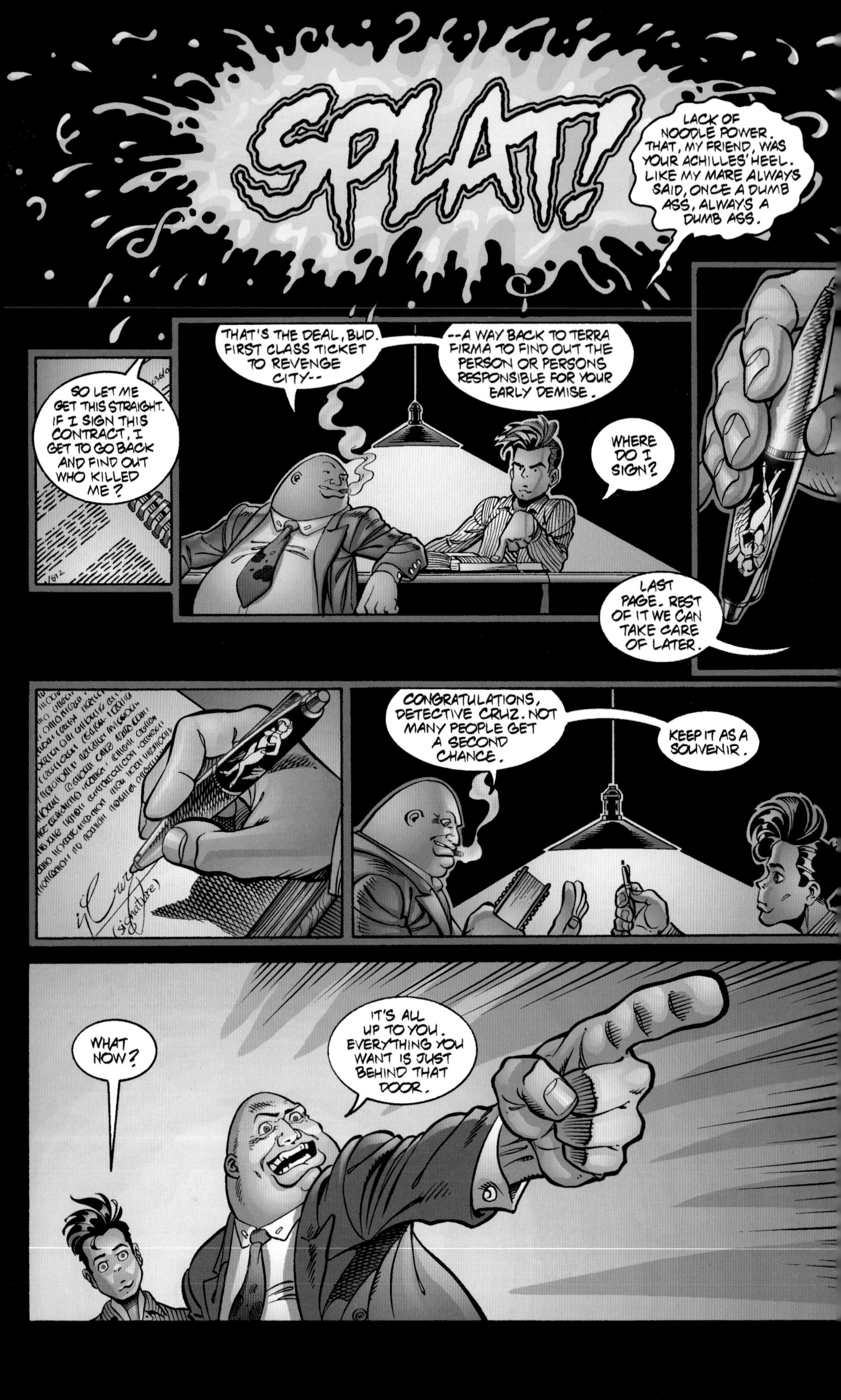
SPLAT!
LACK OF NOODLE POWER. THAT, MY FRIEND, WAS YOUR ACHILLES' HEEL. LIKE MY MARE ALWAYS SAID, ONCE A DUMB ASS, ALWAYS A DUMB ASS.
SO LET ME GET THIS STRAIGHT. IF I SIGN THIS CONTRACT, I GET TO GO BACK AND FIND OUT WHO KILLED ME?
THAT'S THE DEAL, BUD. FIRST CLASS TICKET TO REVENGE CITY--
--A WAY BACK TO TERRA FIRMA TO FIND OUT THE PERSON OR PERSONS RESPONSIBLE FOR YOUR EARLY DEMISE.
WHERE DO I SIGN?
LAST PAGE. REST OF IT WE CAN TAKE CARE OF LATER.
(signature)
CONGRATULATIONS, DETECTIVE CRUZ. NOT MANY PEOPLE GET A SECOND CHANCE.
KEEP IT AS A SOUVENIR.
WHAT NOW?
IT'S ALL UP TO YOU. EVERYTHING YOU WANT IS JUST BEHIND THAT DOOR.

GOOD LUCK...

...SUCKER.

I KNOW WHAT YOU'RE THINKING. WHAT WAS IN THAT CONTRACT? TRUTH IS, I DON'T CARE. I GOT BUSINESS ON THE OTHER SIDE OF THAT DOOR. A FAMILY TO GO HOME TO. I DIDN'T CARE ABOUT THE SMALL PRINT.

WHAT THE *HELL*?

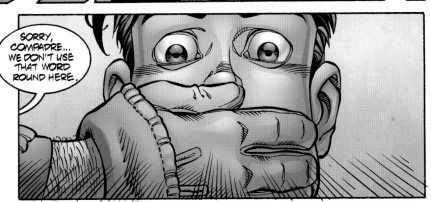

SORRY, COMPADRE... WE DON'T USE THAT WORD ROUND HERE.

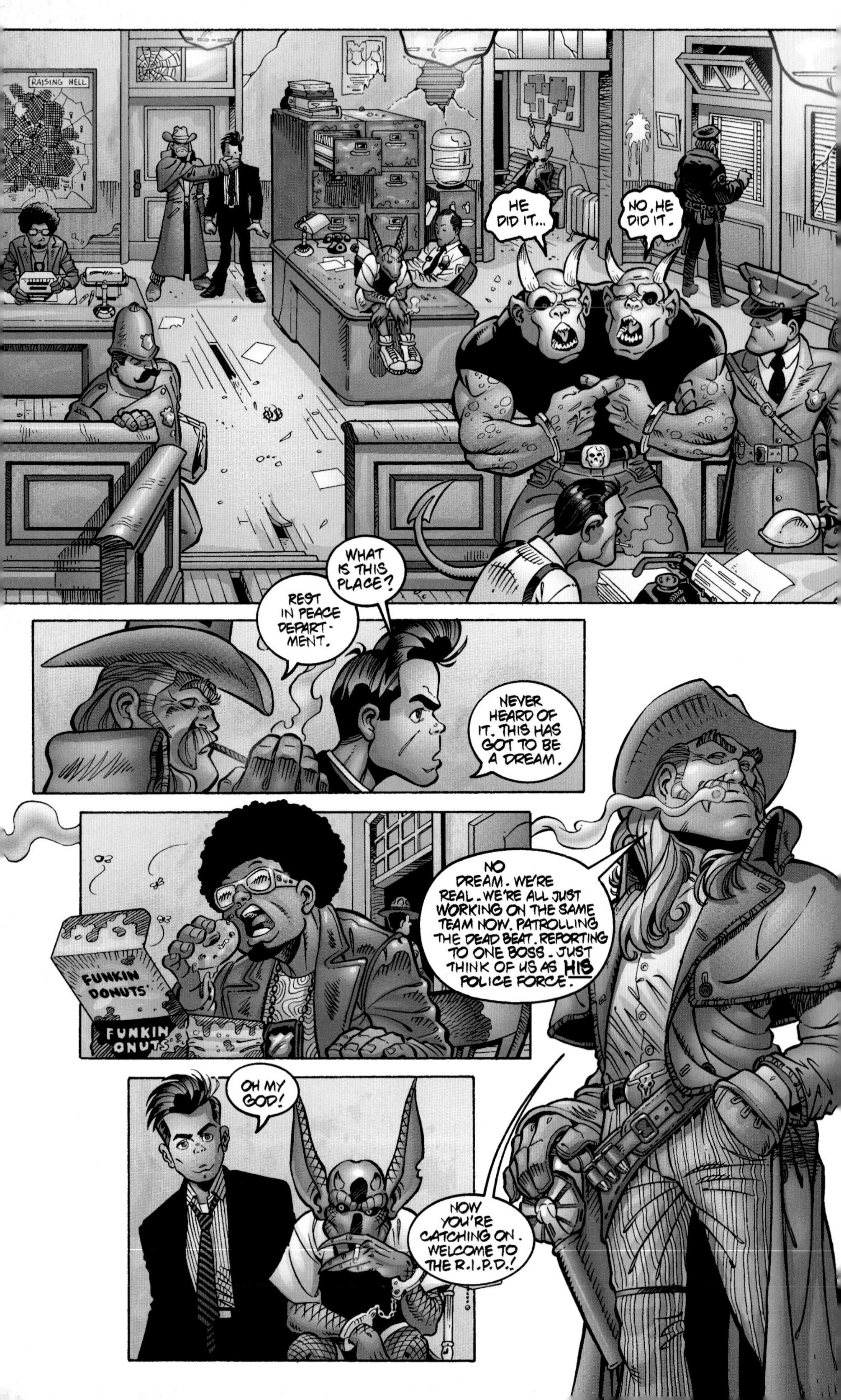
RAISING HELL
HE DID IT...
NO, HE DID IT.
WHAT IS THIS PLACE?
REST IN PEACE DEPART-MENT.
NEVER HEARD OF IT. THIS HAS GOT TO BE A DREAM.
NO DREAM. WE'RE REAL. WE'RE ALL JUST WORKING ON THE SAME TEAM NOW. PATROLLING THE DEAD BEAT. REPORTING TO ONE BOSS. JUST THINK OF US AS HIS POLICE FORCE.
FUNKIN DONUTS
FUNKIN DONUTS
OH MY GOD!
NOW YOU'RE CATCHING ON. WELCOME TO THE R.I.P.D.!

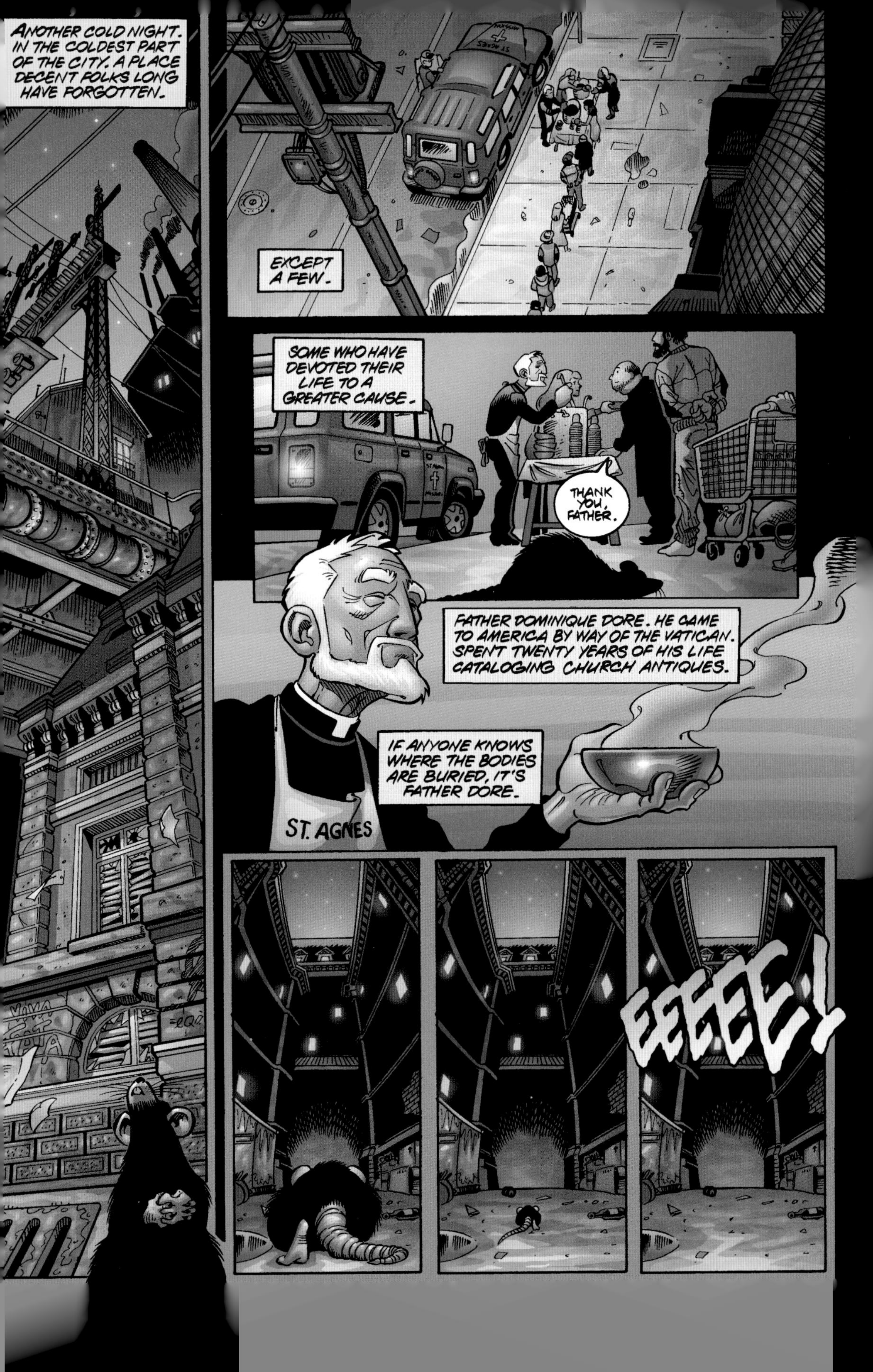
ANOTHER COLD NIGHT. IN THE COLDEST PART OF THE CITY. A PLACE DECENT FOLKS LONG HAVE FORGOTTEN.
EXCEPT A FEW.
SOME WHO HAVE DEVOTED THEIR LIFE TO A GREATER CAUSE.
THANK YOU, FATHER.
FATHER DOMINIQUE DORE. HE CAME TO AMERICA BY WAY OF THE VATICAN. SPENT TWENTY YEARS OF HIS LIFE CATALOGING CHURCH ANTIQUES.
IF ANYONE KNOWS WHERE THE BODIES ARE BURIED, IT'S FATHER DORE.
ST. AGNES
EEEEE!

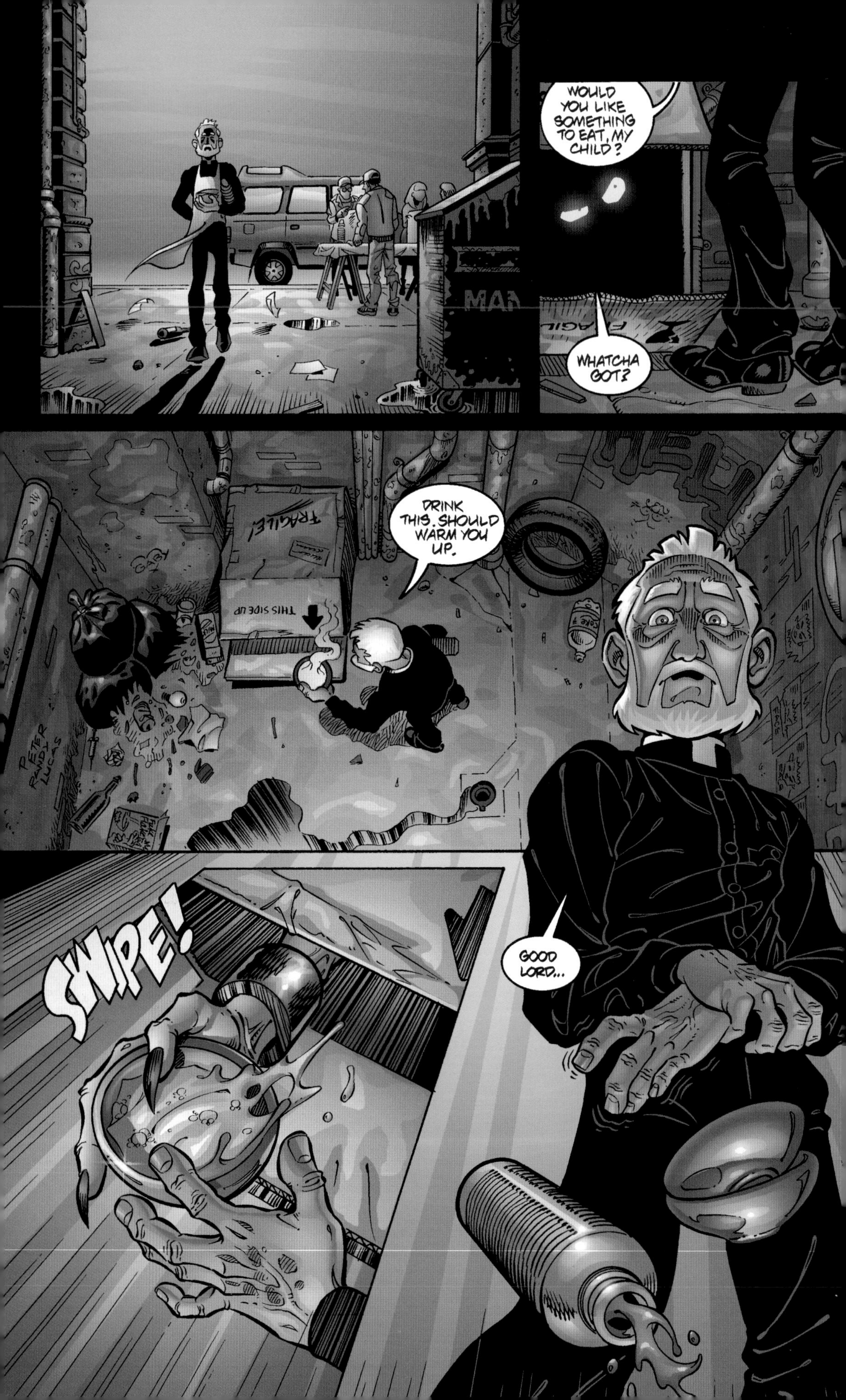
WOULD YOU LIKE SOMETHING TO EAT, MY CHILD?
WHATCHA GOT?
DRINK THIS. SHOULD WARM YOU UP.
SWIPE!
GOOD LORD...

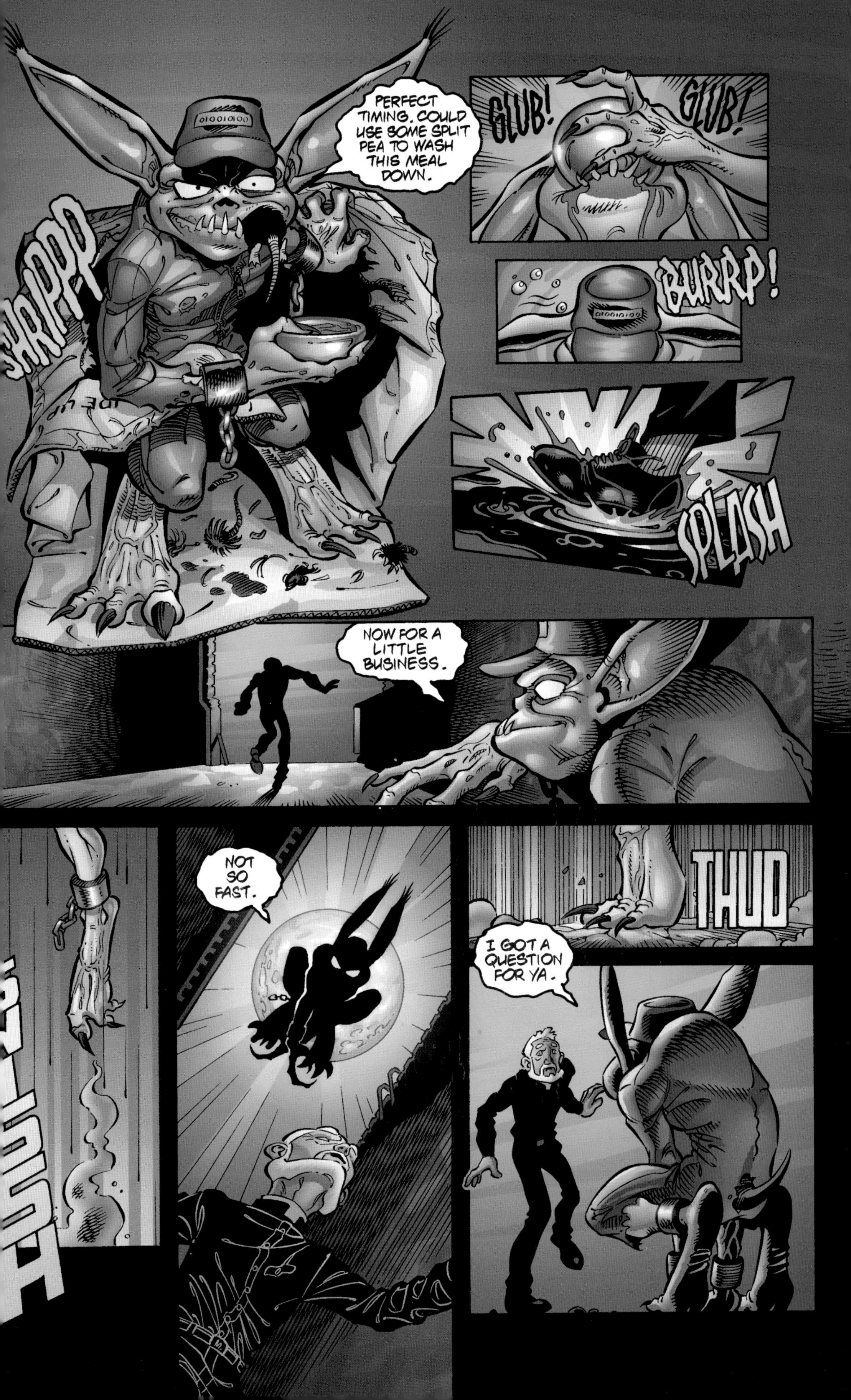
PERFECT TIMING. COULD USE SOME SPLIT PEA TO WASH THIS MEAL DOWN.
SHRIPPP
GLUB!
GLUB!
BURRP!
SPLASH
NOW FOR A LITTLE BUSINESS.
NOT SO FAST.
THUD
I GOT A QUESTION FOR YA.

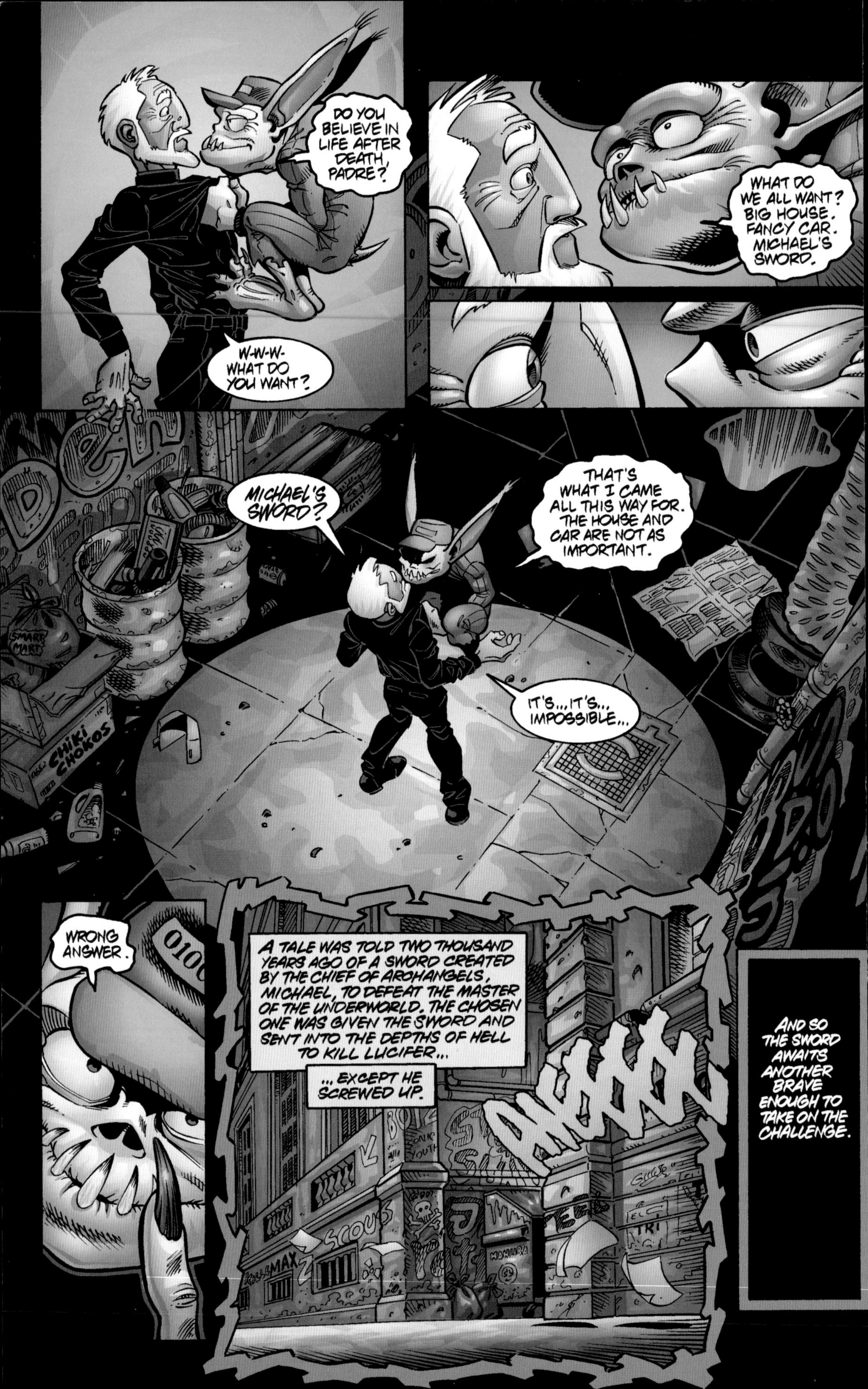
DO YOU BELIEVE IN LIFE AFTER DEATH, PADRE?
W-W-W- WHAT DO YOU WANT?
WHAT DO WE ALL WANT? BIG HOUSE. FANCY CAR. MICHAEL'S SWORD.
MICHAEL'S SWORD?
THAT'S WHAT I CAME ALL THIS WAY FOR. THE HOUSE AND CAR ARE NOT AS IMPORTANT.
IT'S... IT'S... IMPOSSIBLE...
SMART MART
CHIKI CHOKOS
WRONG ANSWER.
A TALE WAS TOLD TWO THOUSAND YEARS AGO OF A SWORD CREATED BY THE CHIEF OF ARCHANGELS, MICHAEL, TO DEFEAT THE MASTER OF THE UNDERWORLD. THE CHOSEN ONE WAS GIVEN THE SWORD AND SENT INTO THE DEPTHS OF HELL TO KILL LUCIFER...
... EXCEPT HE SCREWED UP.
SONIC YOUTH
SCOUTS
MAX
AND SO THE SWORD AWAITS ANOTHER BRAVE ENOUGH TO TAKE ON THE CHALLENGE.

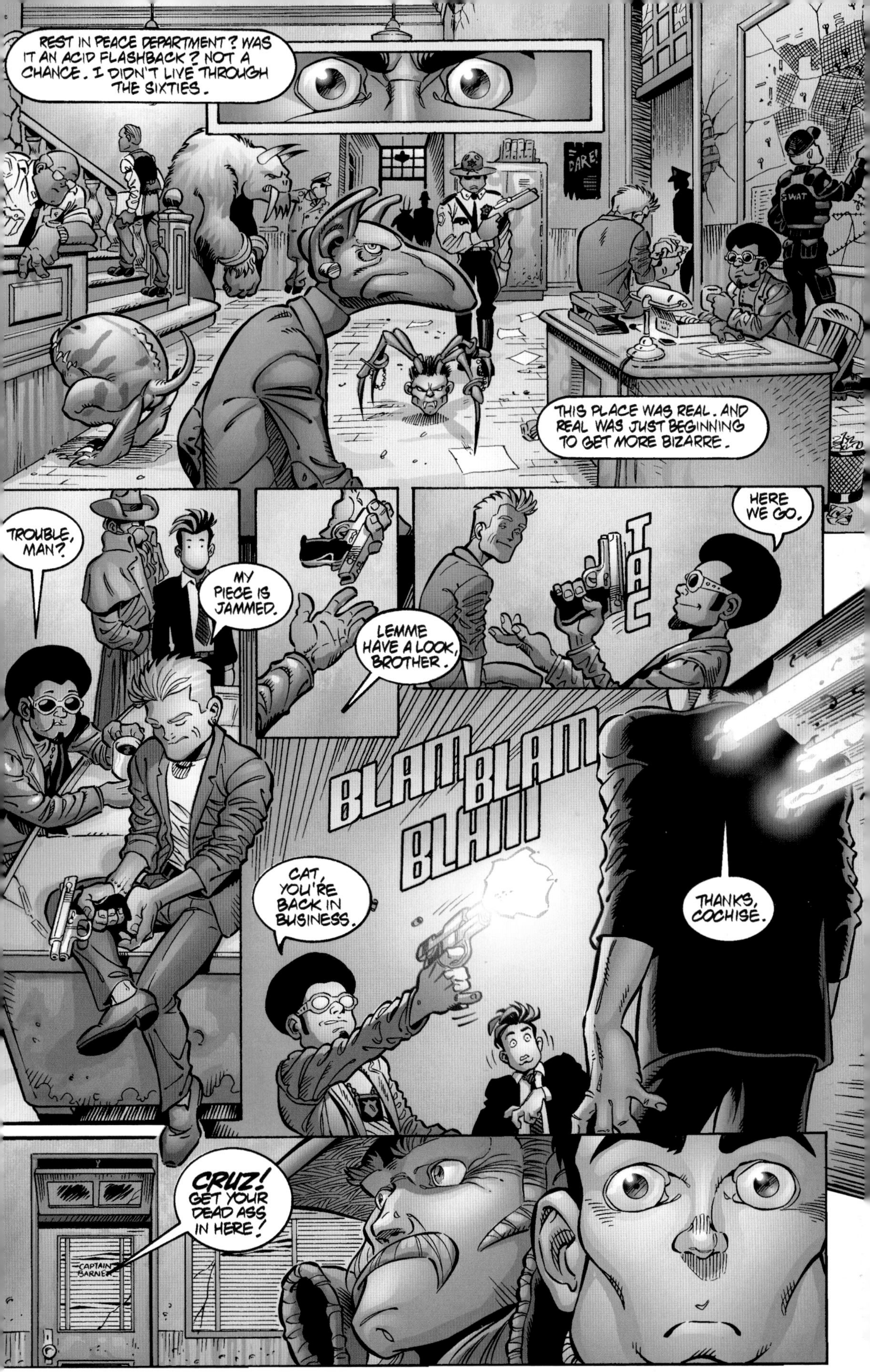
REST IN PEACE DEPARTMENT? WAS IT AN ACID FLASHBACK? NOT A CHANCE. I DIDN'T LIVE THROUGH THE SIXTIES.
DARE!
SWAT
THIS PLACE WAS REAL. AND REAL WAS JUST BEGINNING TO GET MORE BIZARRE.
TROUBLE, MAN?
MY PIECE IS JAMMED.
LEMME HAVE A LOOK, BROTHER.
HERE WE GO.
TAC
BLAM BLAM BLAM
CAT, YOU'RE BACK IN BUSINESS.
THANKS, COCHISE.
CAPTAIN BARNES
CRUZ! GET YOUR DEAD ASS IN HERE!

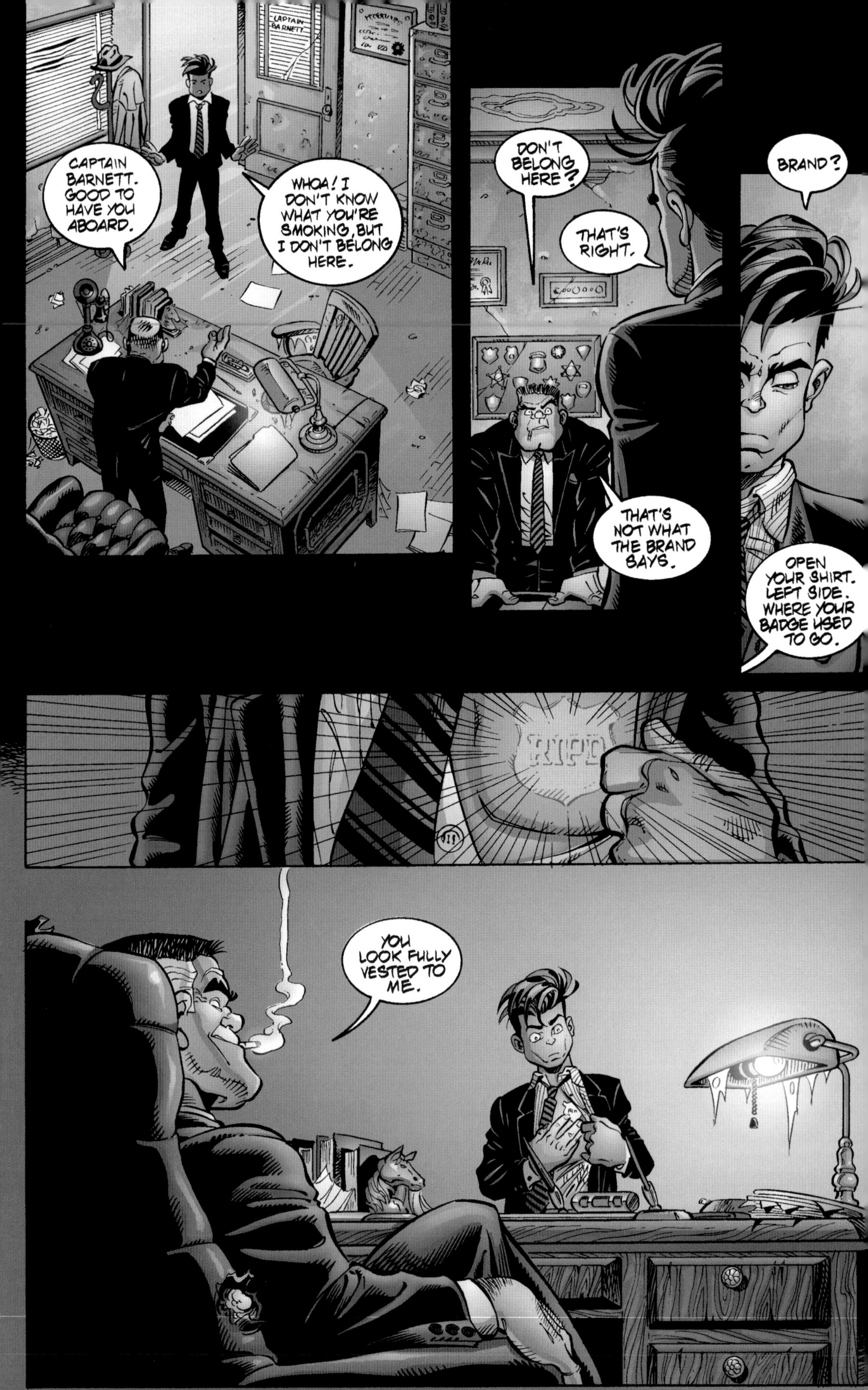
CAPTAIN BARNETT. GOOD TO HAVE YOU ABOARD.
WHOA! I DON'T KNOW WHAT YOU'RE SMOKING, BUT I DON'T BELONG HERE.
DON'T BELONG HERE?
THAT'S RIGHT.
THAT'S NOT WHAT THE BRAND SAYS.
BRAND?
OPEN YOUR SHIRT. LEFT SIDE. WHERE YOUR BADGE USED TO GO.
RIPD
YOU LOOK FULLY VESTED TO ME.

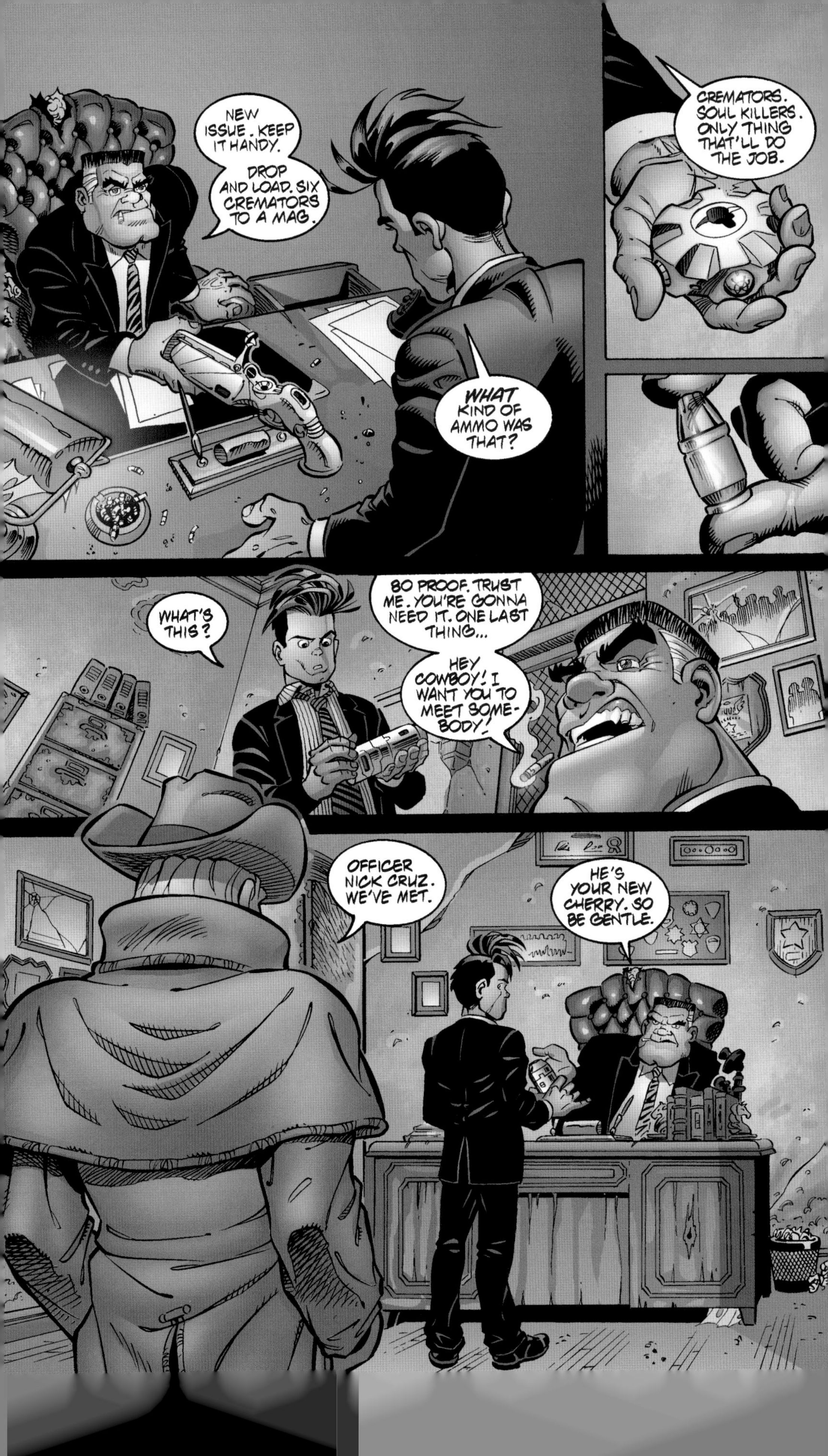
NEW ISSUE. KEEP IT HANDY.
DROP AND LOAD. SIX CREMATORS TO A MAG.
CREMATORS. SOUL KILLERS. ONLY THING THAT'LL DO THE JOB.
WHAT KIND OF AMMO WAS THAT?
WHAT'S THIS?
80 PROOF. TRUST ME. YOU'RE GONNA NEED IT. ONE LAST THING...
HEY COWBOY! I WANT YOU TO MEET SOMEBODY!
OFFICER NICK CRUZ. WE'VE MET.
HE'S YOUR NEW CHERRY. SO BE GENTLE.

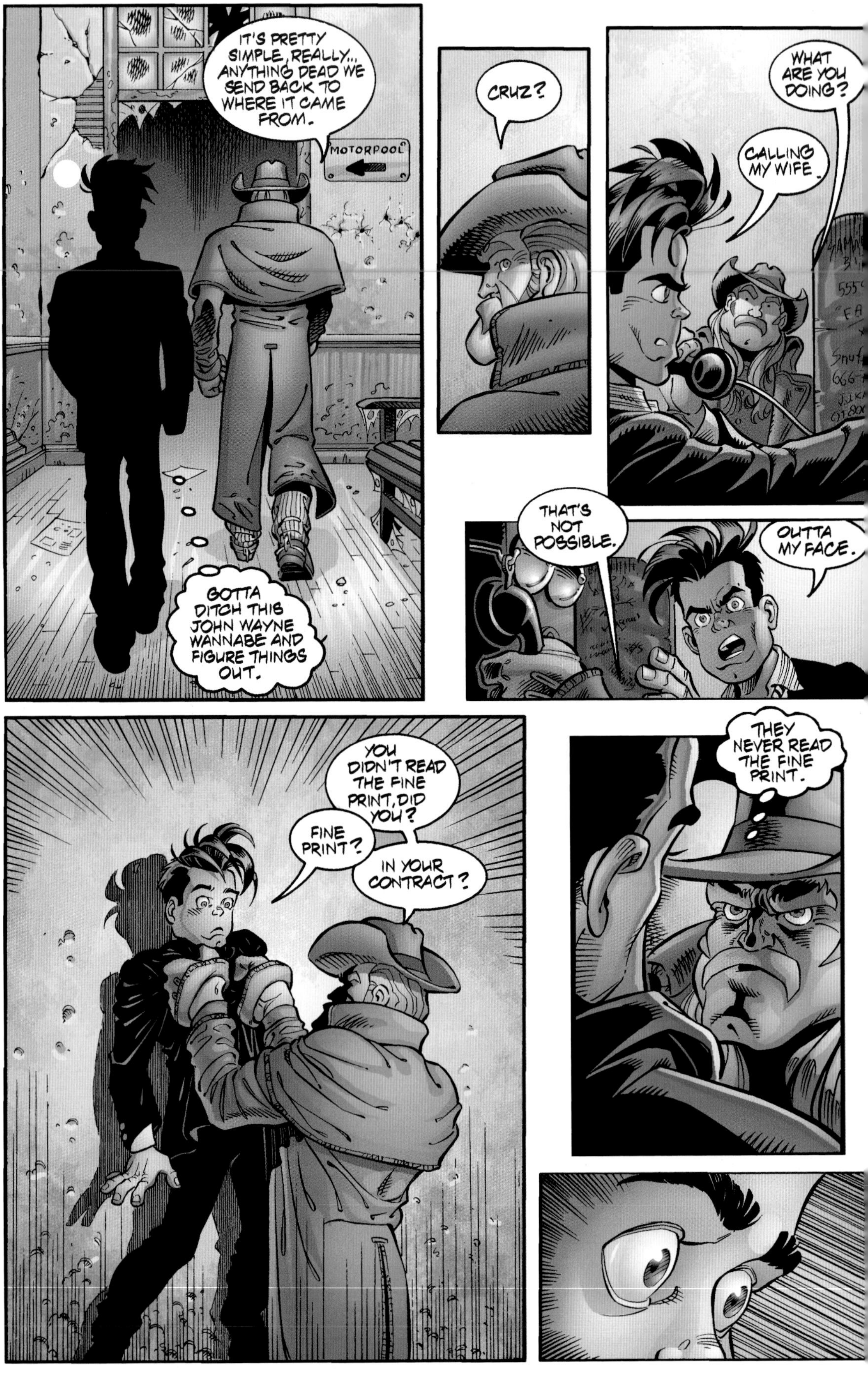

IT'S PRETTY SIMPLE, REALLY... ANYTHING DEAD WE SEND BACK TO WHERE IT CAME FROM.
MOTORPOOL
GOTTA DITCH THIS JOHN WAYNE WANNABE AND FIGURE THINGS OUT.
CRUZ?
WHAT ARE YOU DOING?
CALLING MY WIFE.
THAT'S NOT POSSIBLE.
OUTTA MY FACE.
YOU DIDN'T READ THE FINE PRINT, DID YOU?
FINE PRINT?
IN YOUR CONTRACT?
THEY NEVER READ THE FINE PRINT.

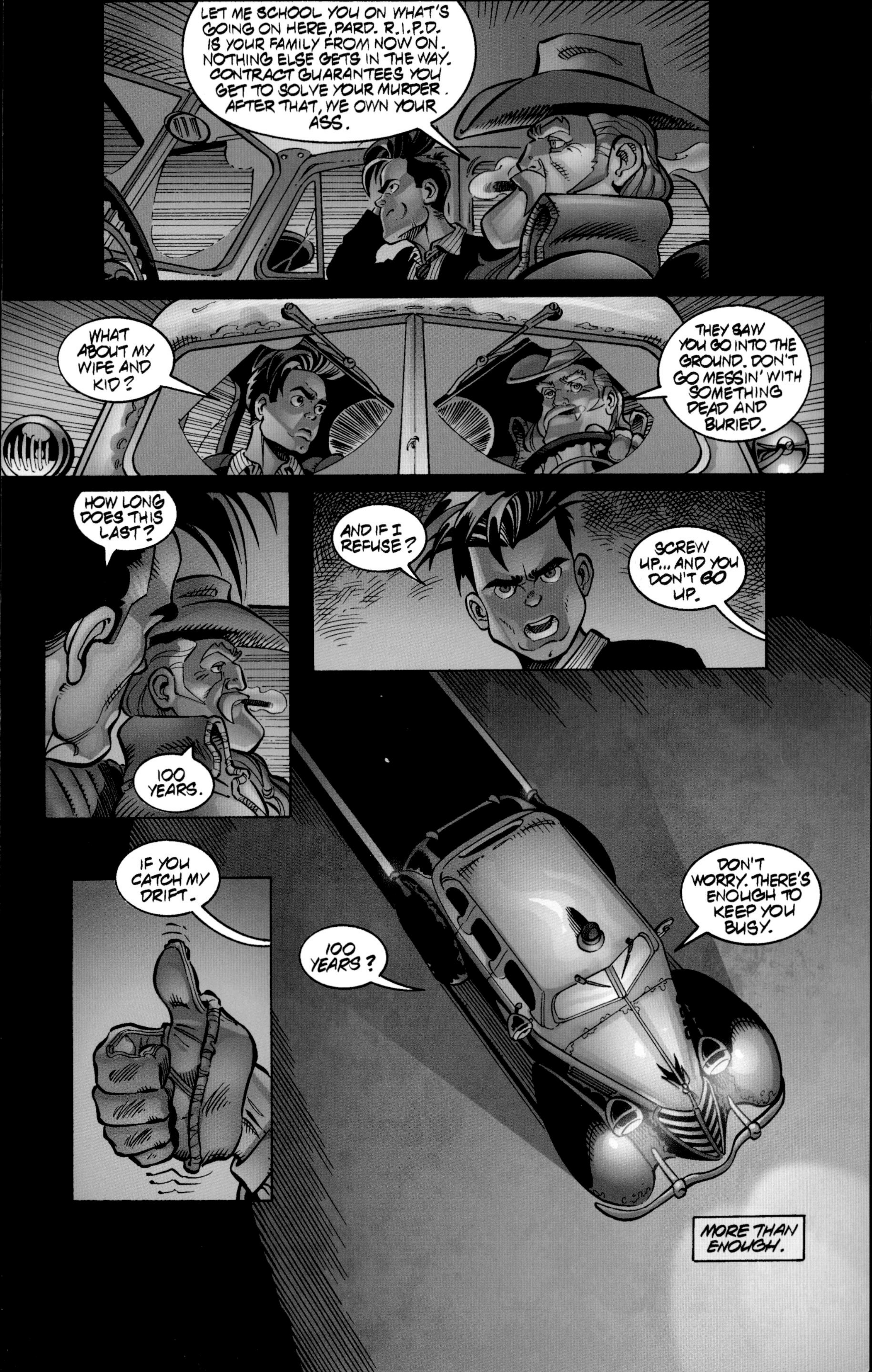
LET ME SCHOOL YOU ON WHAT'S GOING ON HERE, PARD. R.I.P.D. IS YOUR FAMILY FROM NOW ON. NOTHING ELSE GETS IN THE WAY. CONTRACT GUARANTEES YOU GET TO SOLVE YOUR MURDER. AFTER THAT, WE OWN YOUR ASS.
WHAT ABOUT MY WIFE AND KID?
THEY SAW YOU GO INTO THE GROUND. DON'T GO MESSIN' WITH SOMETHING DEAD AND BURIED.
HOW LONG DOES THIS LAST?
100 YEARS.
AND IF I REFUSE?
SCREW UP... AND YOU DON'T GO UP.
IF YOU CATCH MY DRIFT.
100 YEARS?
DON'T WORRY. THERE'S ENOUGH TO KEEP YOU BUSY.
MORE THAN ENOUGH.

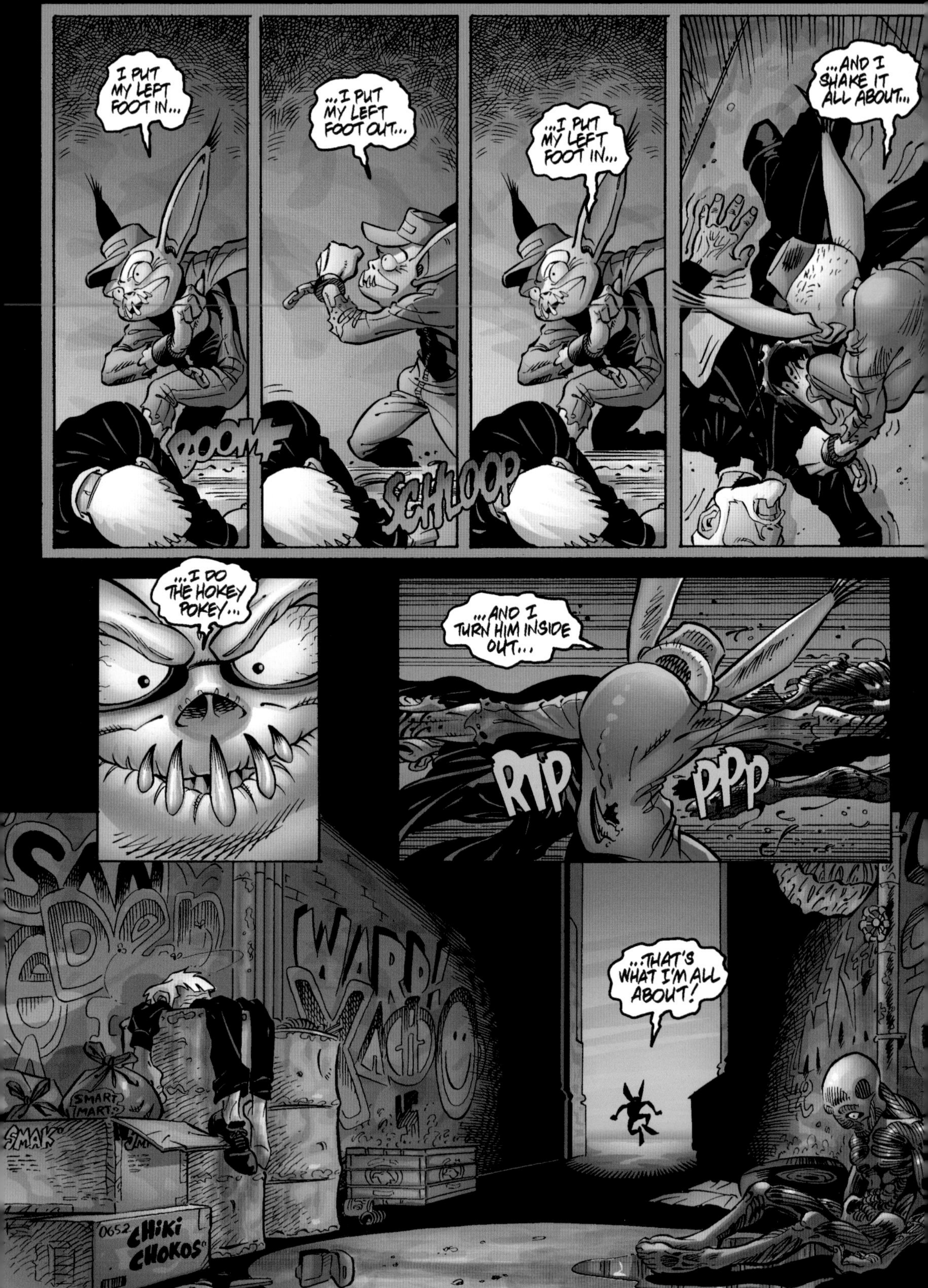
I PUT MY LEFT FOOT IN...
DOOMF
...I PUT MY LEFT FOOT OUT...
SCHLOOP
...I PUT MY LEFT FOOT IN...
...AND I SHAKE IT ALL ABOUT...
...I DO THE HOKEY POKEY...
...AND I TURN HIM INSIDE OUT...
RIP
PPP
SMAK
WARD!
SMART MART
CHIKI CHOKOS
0652
...THAT'S WHAT I'M ALL ABOUT!

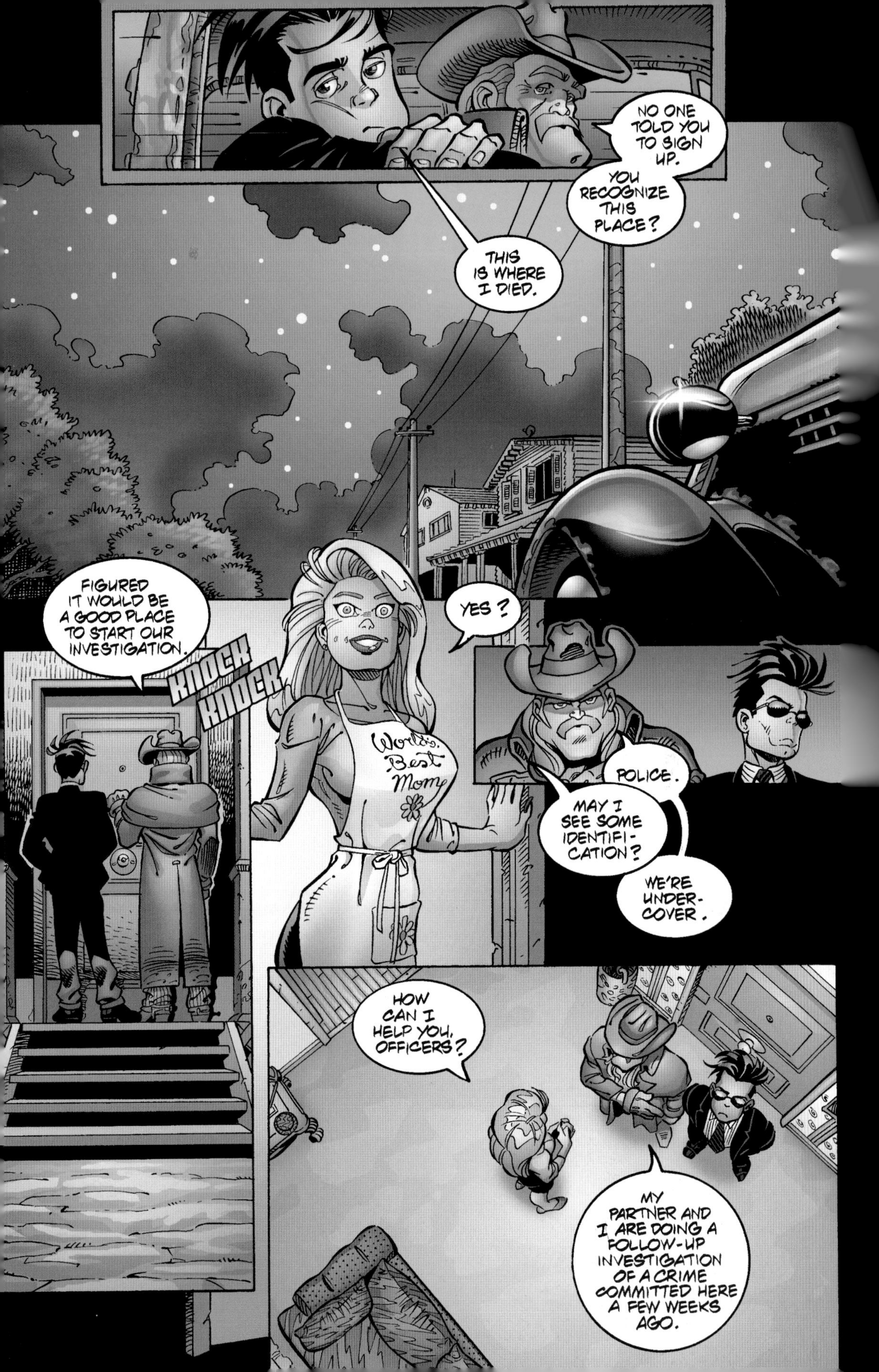
NO ONE TOLD YOU TO SIGN UP.
YOU RECOGNIZE THIS PLACE?
THIS IS WHERE I DIED.
FIGURED IT WOULD BE A GOOD PLACE TO START OUR INVESTIGATION.
KNOCK KNOCK
YES?
World's Best Mom
POLICE.
MAY I SEE SOME IDENTIFI-CATION?
WE'RE UNDER-COVER.
HOW CAN I HELP YOU, OFFICERS?
MY PARTNER AND I ARE DOING A FOLLOW-UP INVESTIGATION OF A CRIME COMMITTED HERE A FEW WEEKS AGO.

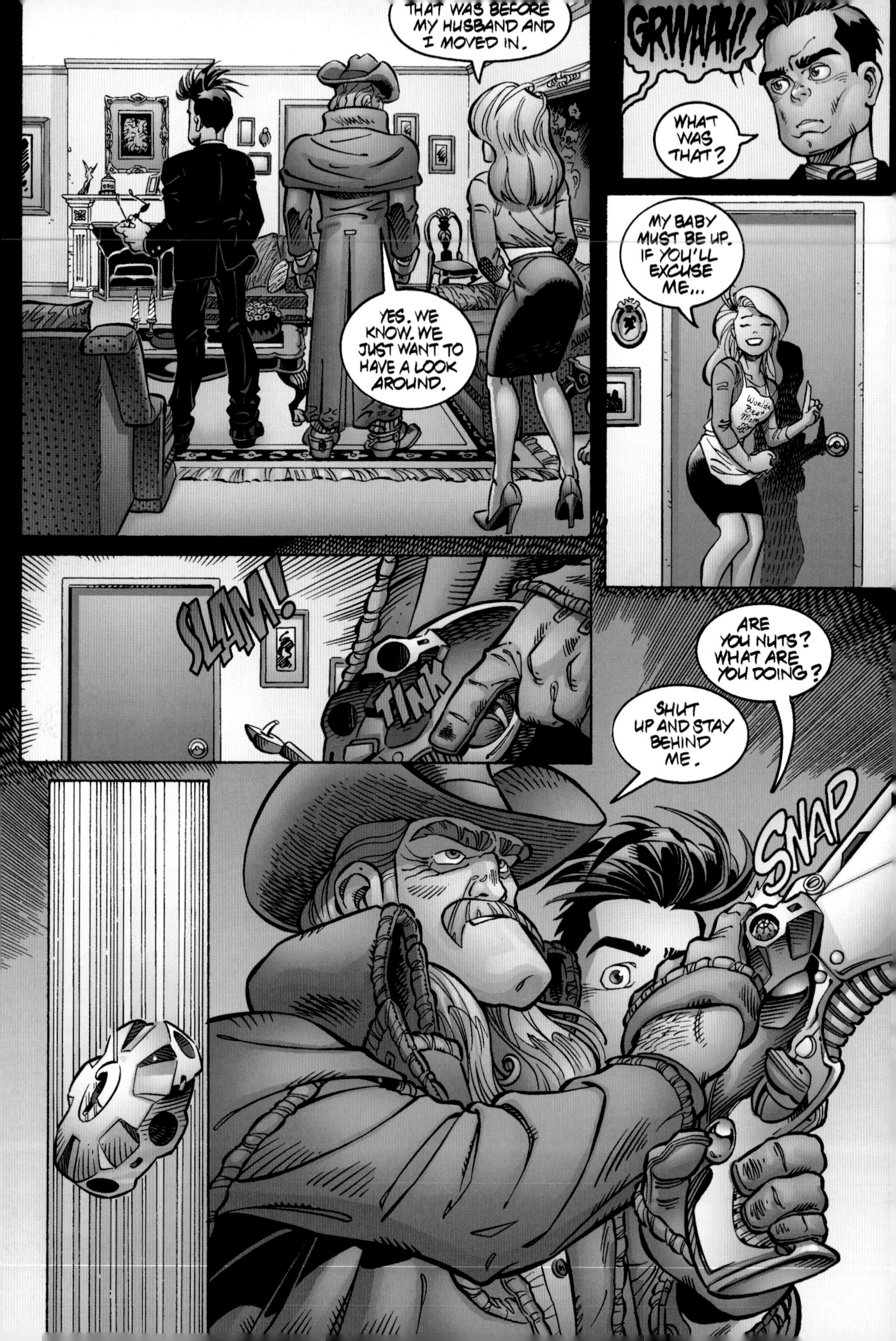
THAT WAS BEFORE MY HUSBAND AND I MOVED IN.
YES. WE KNOW. WE JUST WANT TO HAVE A LOOK AROUND.
GRWAAH!!
WHAT WAS THAT?
MY BABY MUST BE UP. IF YOU'LL EXCUSE ME...
SLAM!
TINK
ARE YOU NUTS? WHAT ARE YOU DOING?
SHUT UP AND STAY BEHIND ME.
SNAP

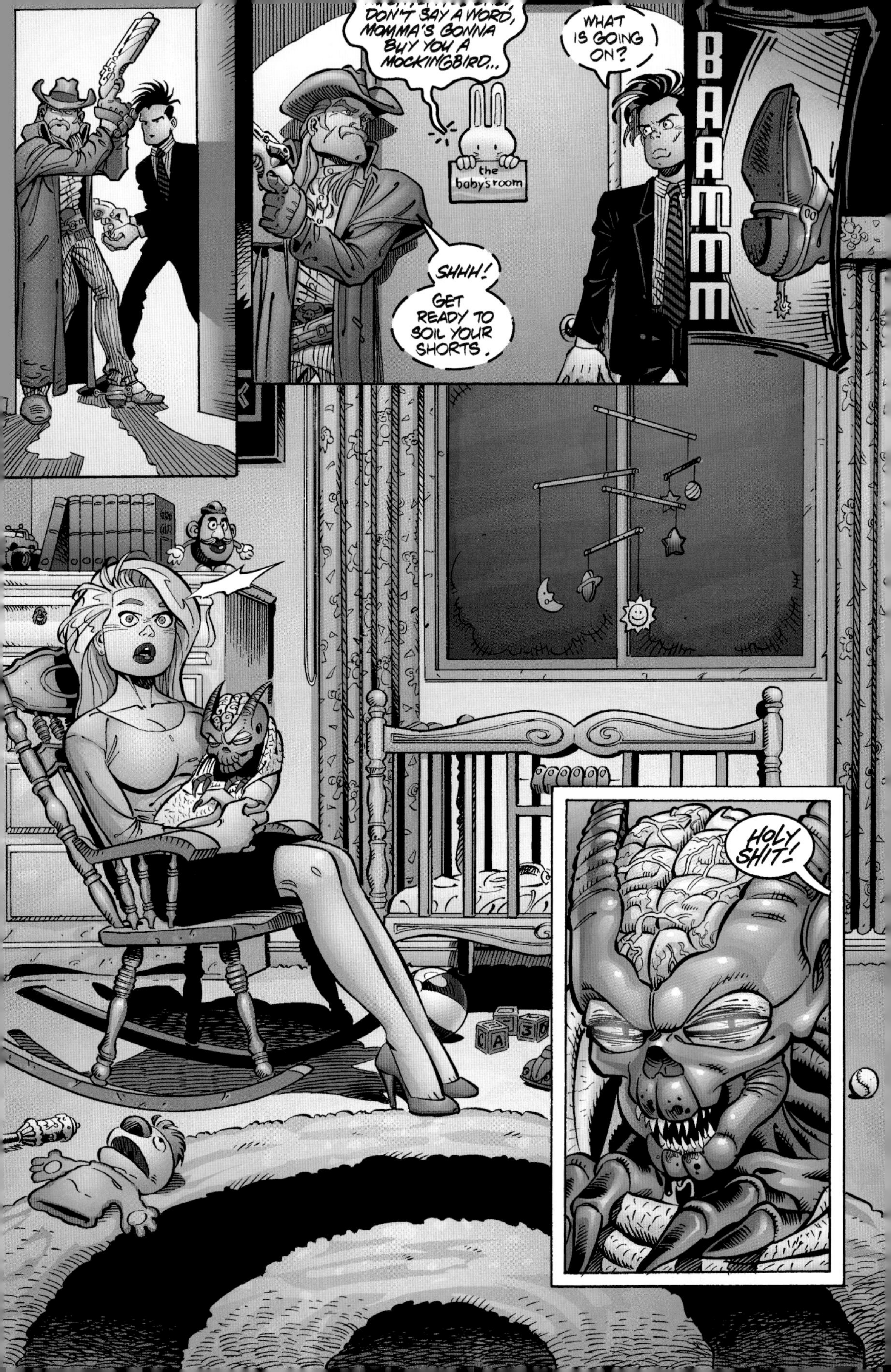
DON'T SAY A WORD, MOMMA'S GONNA BUY YOU A MOCKINGBIRD...
the baby's room
SHHH!
GET READY TO SOIL YOUR SHORTS.
WHAT IS GOING ON?
BAAMMM
HOLY SHIT!

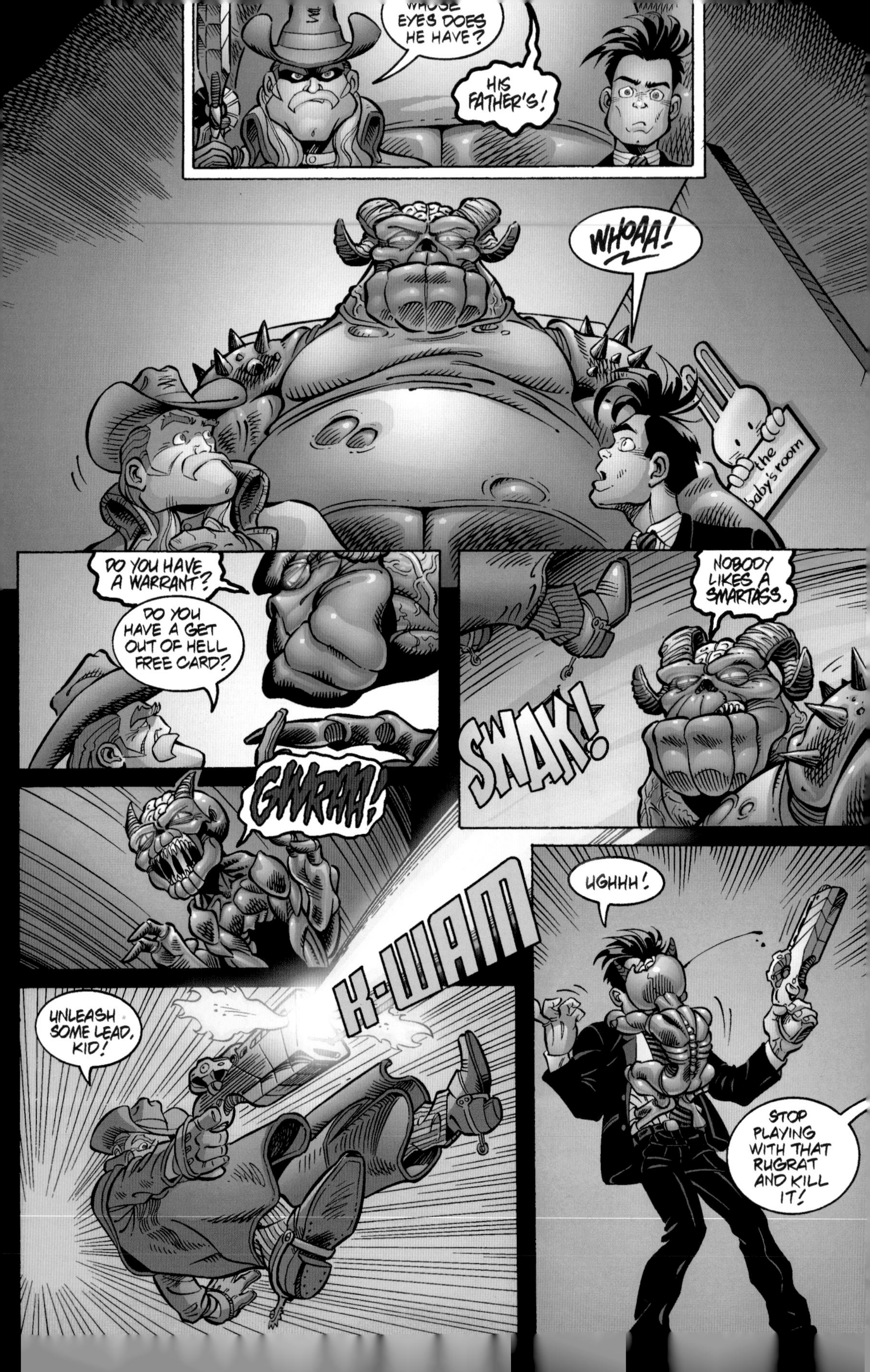
WHOSE EYES DOES HE HAVE?
HIS FATHER'S!
WHOAA!
the baby's room
DO YOU HAVE A WARRANT?
DO YOU HAVE A GET OUT OF HELL FREE CARD?
NOBODY LIKES A SMARTASS.
SNAK!
GWRAAA!
K-WAM
UGHHH!
UNLEASH SOME LEAD, KID!
STOP PLAYING WITH THAT RUGRAT AND KILL IT!

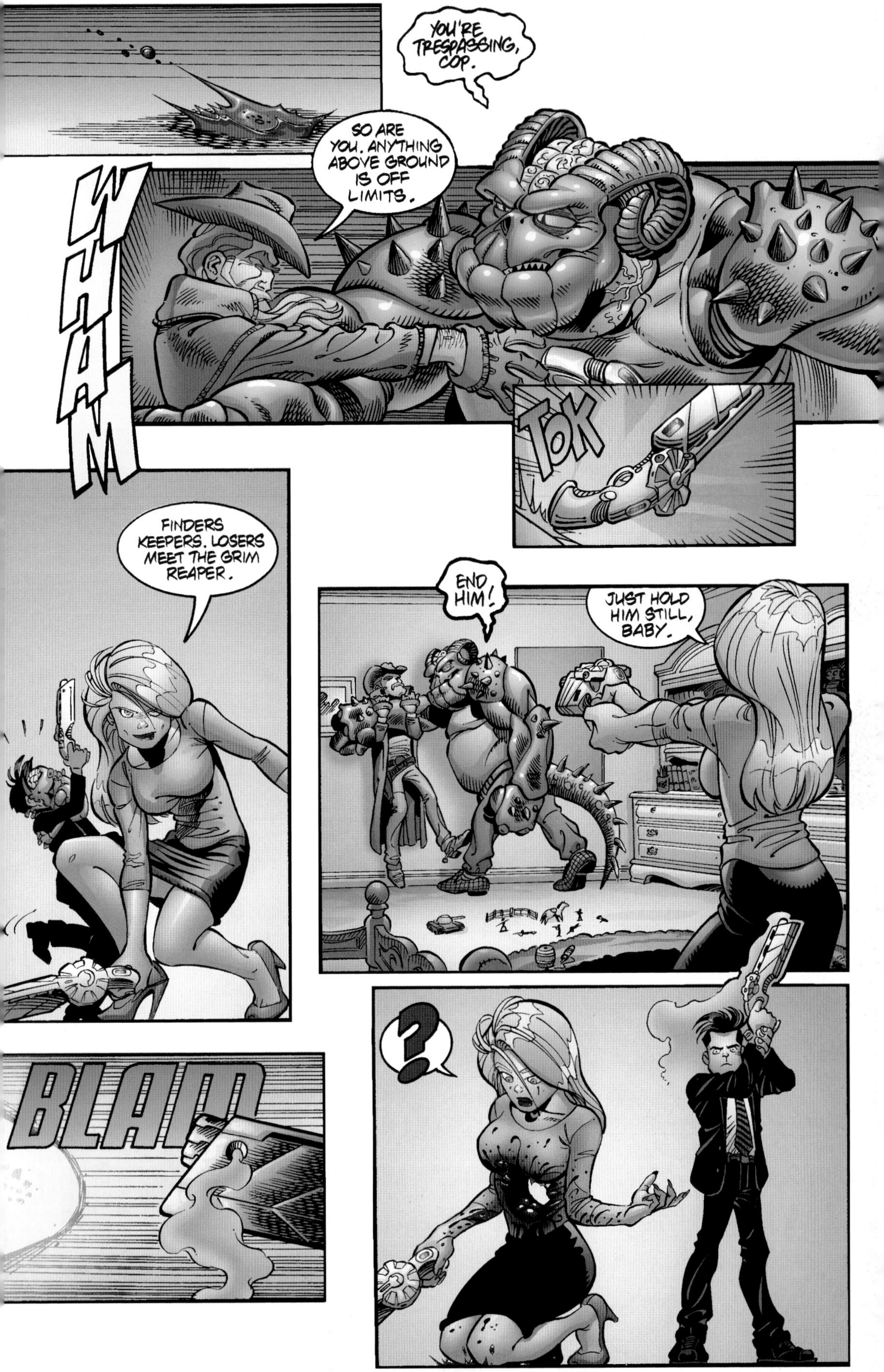
YOU'RE TRESPASSING, COP.
SO ARE YOU. ANYTHING ABOVE GROUND IS OFF LIMITS.
WHAM
TOK
FINDERS KEEPERS. LOSERS MEET THE GRIM REAPER.
END HIM!
JUST HOLD HIM STILL, BABY.
BLAM
?

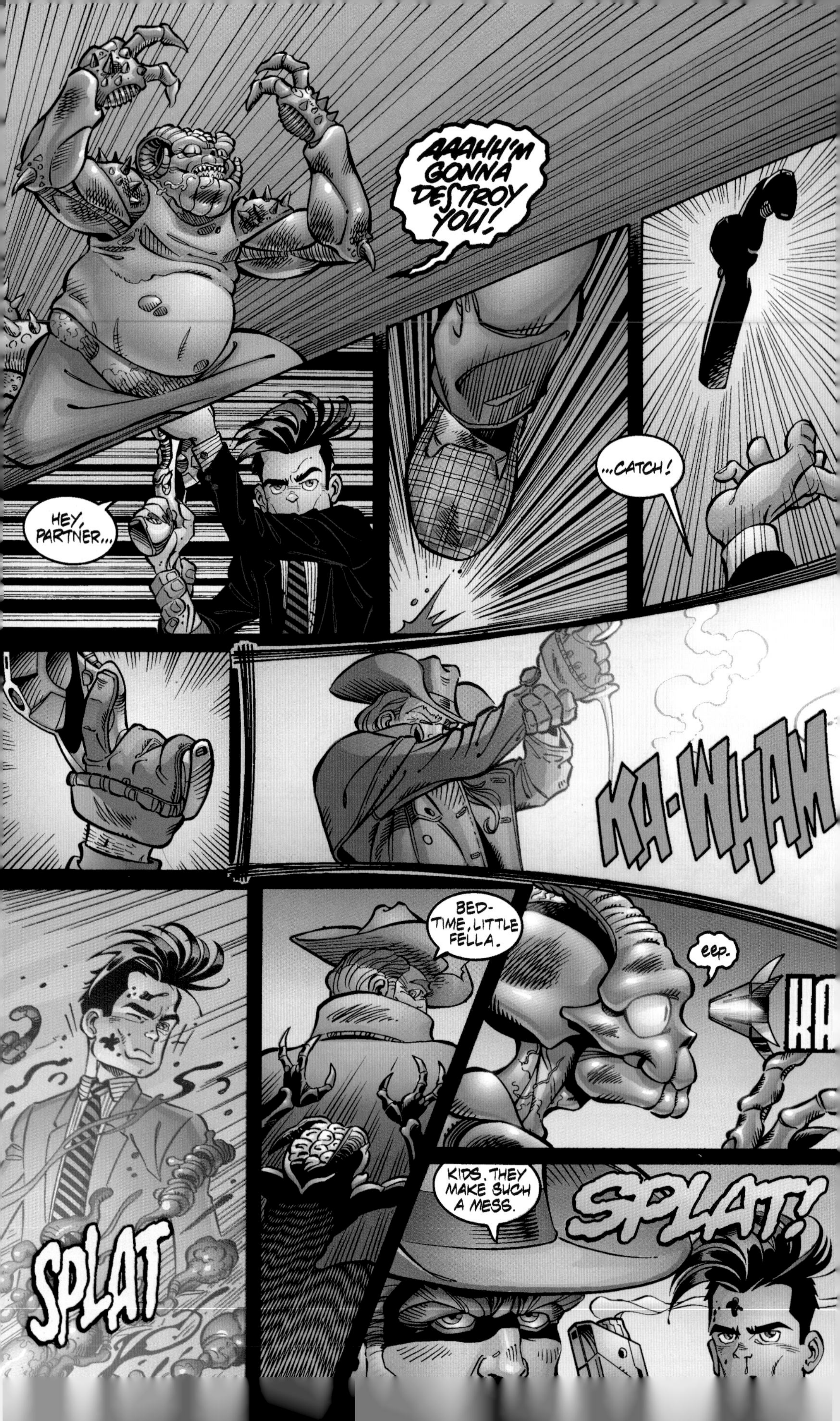
AAAHH'M GONNA DESTROY YOU!
HEY, PARTNER...
...CATCH!
KA-WHAM
BED-TIME, LITTLE FELLA.
eep.
SPLAT
KIDS. THEY MAKE SUCH A MESS.
SPLAT!

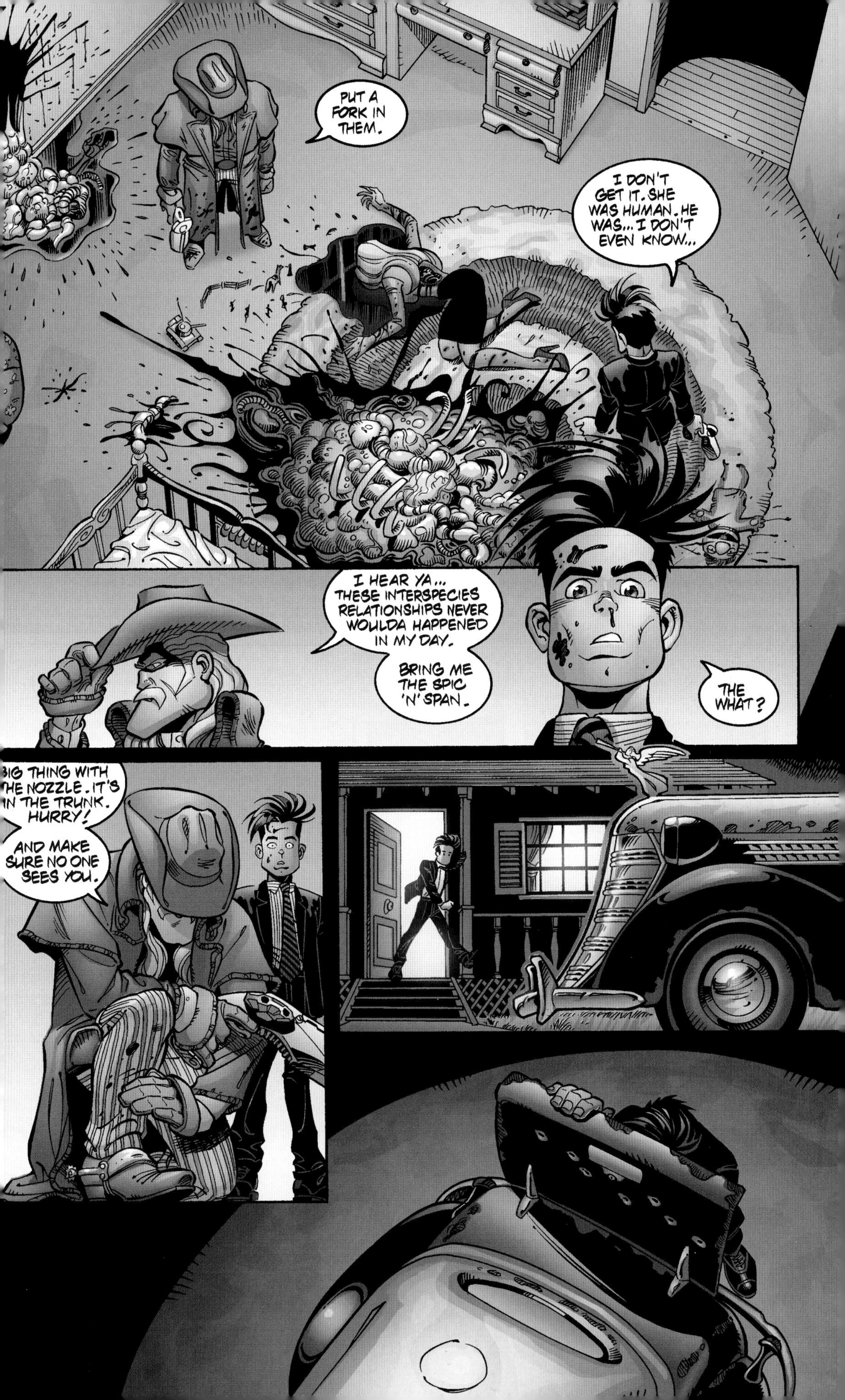
PUT A FORK IN THEM.
I DON'T GET IT. SHE WAS HUMAN. HE WAS... I DON'T EVEN KNOW...
I HEAR YA... THESE INTERSPECIES RELATIONSHIPS NEVER WOULDA HAPPENED IN MY DAY.
BRING ME THE SPIC 'N' SPAN.
THE WHAT?
BIG THING WITH THE NOZZLE. IT'S IN THE TRUNK. HURRY!
AND MAKE SURE NO ONE SEES YOU.

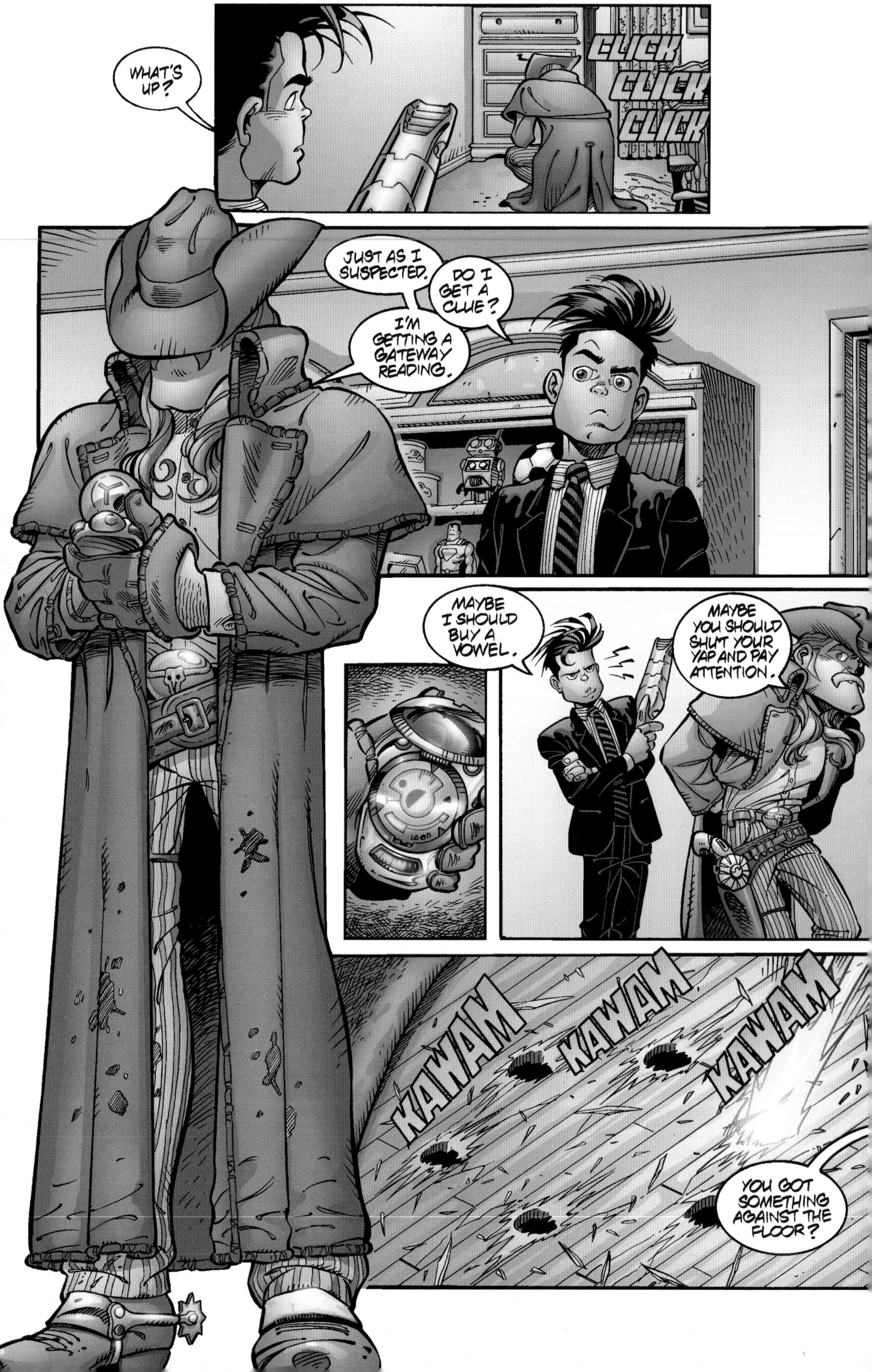
WHAT'S UP?
CLICK
CLICK
CLICK
JUST AS I SUSPECTED.
DO I GET A CLUE?
I'M GETTING A GATEWAY READING.
MAYBE I SHOULD BUY A VOWEL.
MAYBE YOU SHOULD SHUT YOUR YAP AND PAY ATTENTION.
KAWAM
KAWAM
KAWAM
YOU GOT SOMETHING AGAINST THE FLOOR?

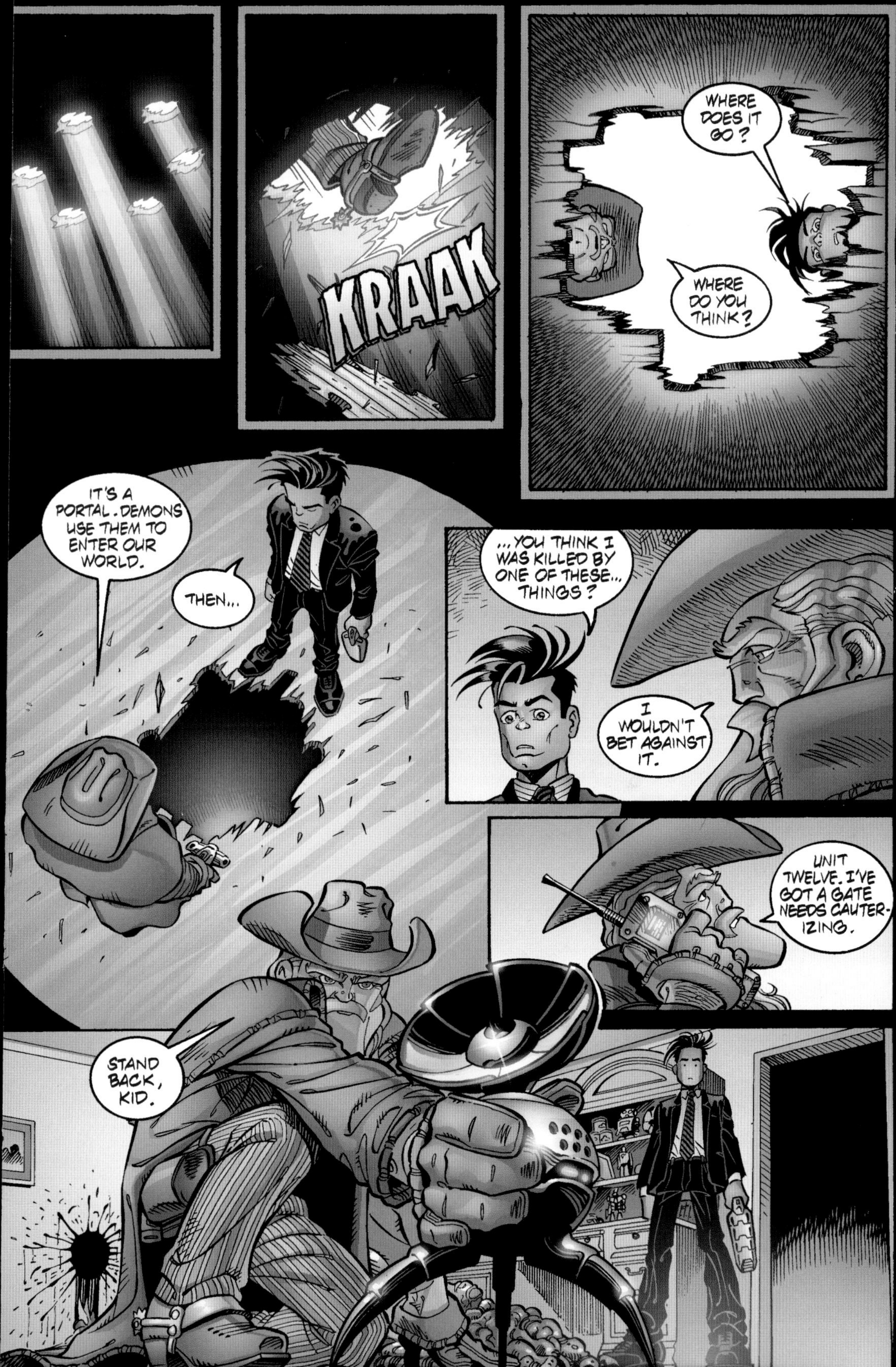
KRAAK
WHERE DOES IT GO?
WHERE DO YOU THINK?
IT'S A PORTAL. DEMONS USE THEM TO ENTER OUR WORLD.
THEN...
...YOU THINK I WAS KILLED BY ONE OF THESE... THINGS?
I WOULDN'T BET AGAINST IT.
UNIT TWELVE. I'VE GOT A GATE NEEDS CAUTER-IZING.
STAND BACK, KID.

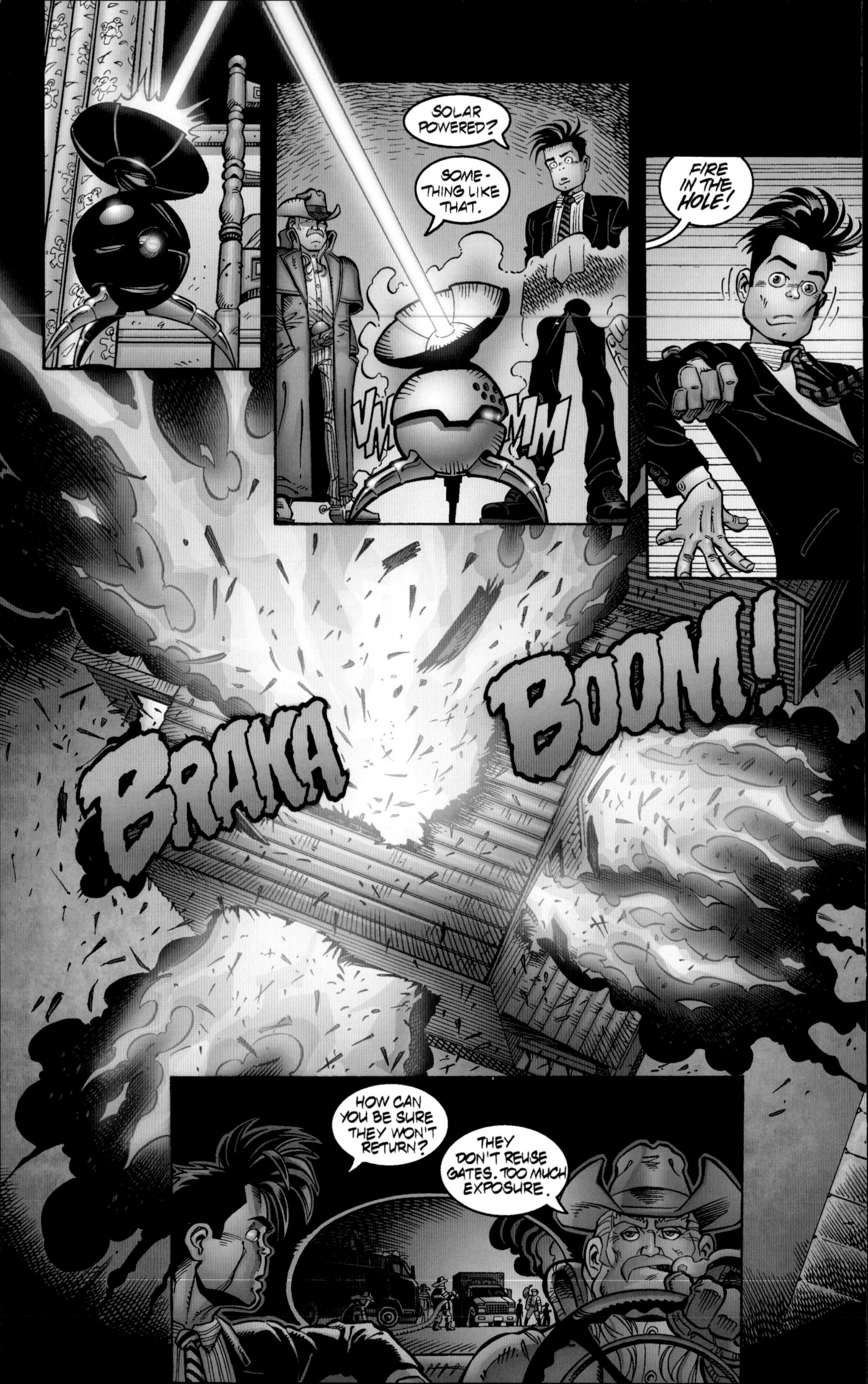
SOLAR POWERED?
SOME-THING LIKE THAT.
VMMMM
FIRE IN THE HOLE!
BRAKA
BOOM!
HOW CAN YOU BE SURE THEY WON'T RETURN?
THEY DON'T REUSE GATES. TOO MUCH EXPOSURE.

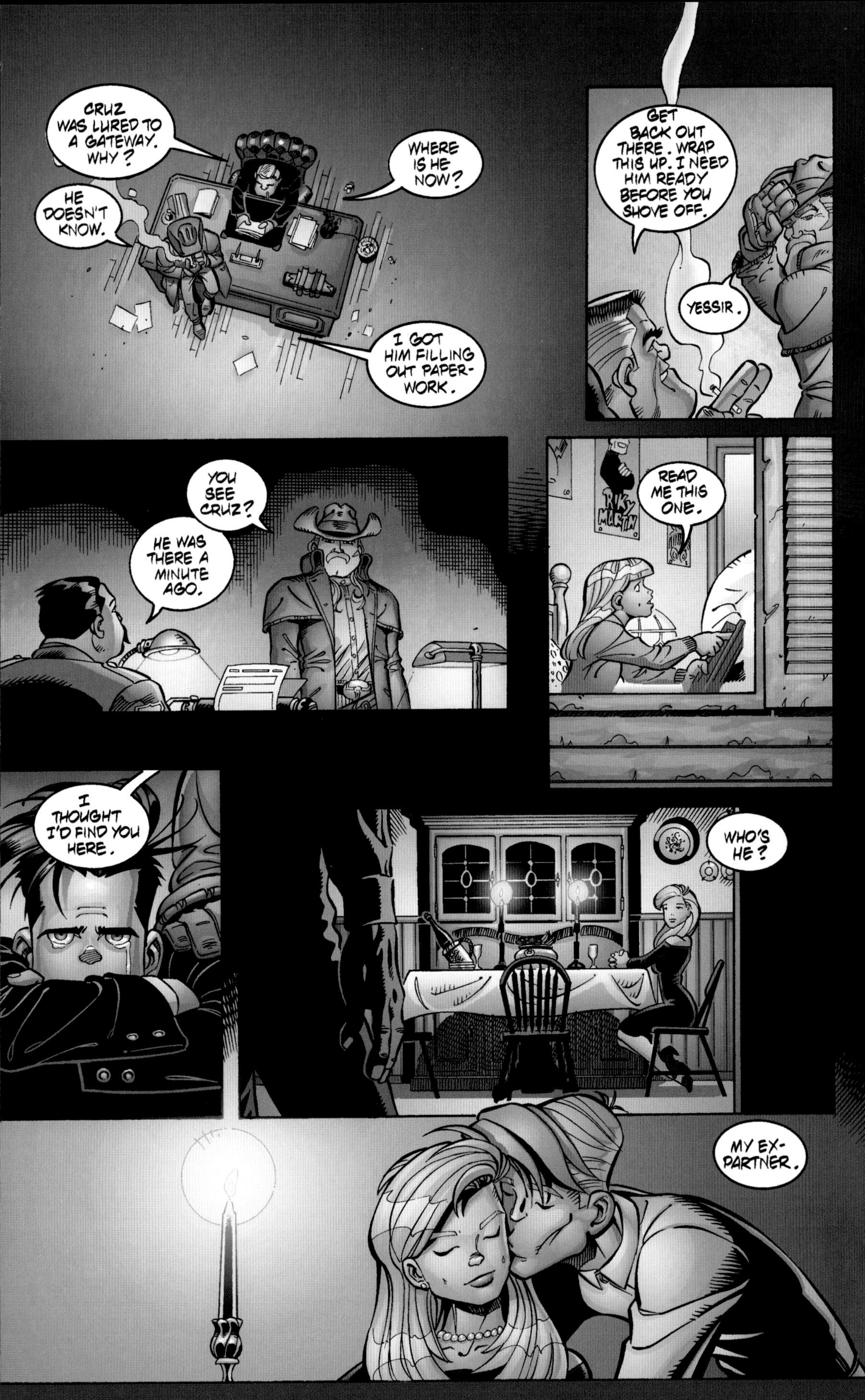
CRUZ WAS LURED TO A GATEWAY. WHY?
HE DOESN'T KNOW.
WHERE IS HE NOW?
I GOT HIM FILLING OUT PAPER-WORK.
GET BACK OUT THERE. WRAP THIS UP. I NEED HIM READY BEFORE YOU SHOVE OFF.
YESSIR.
YOU SEE CRUZ?
HE WAS THERE A MINUTE AGO.
READ ME THIS ONE.
I THOUGHT I'D FIND YOU HERE.
WHO'S HE?
MY EX-PARTNER.

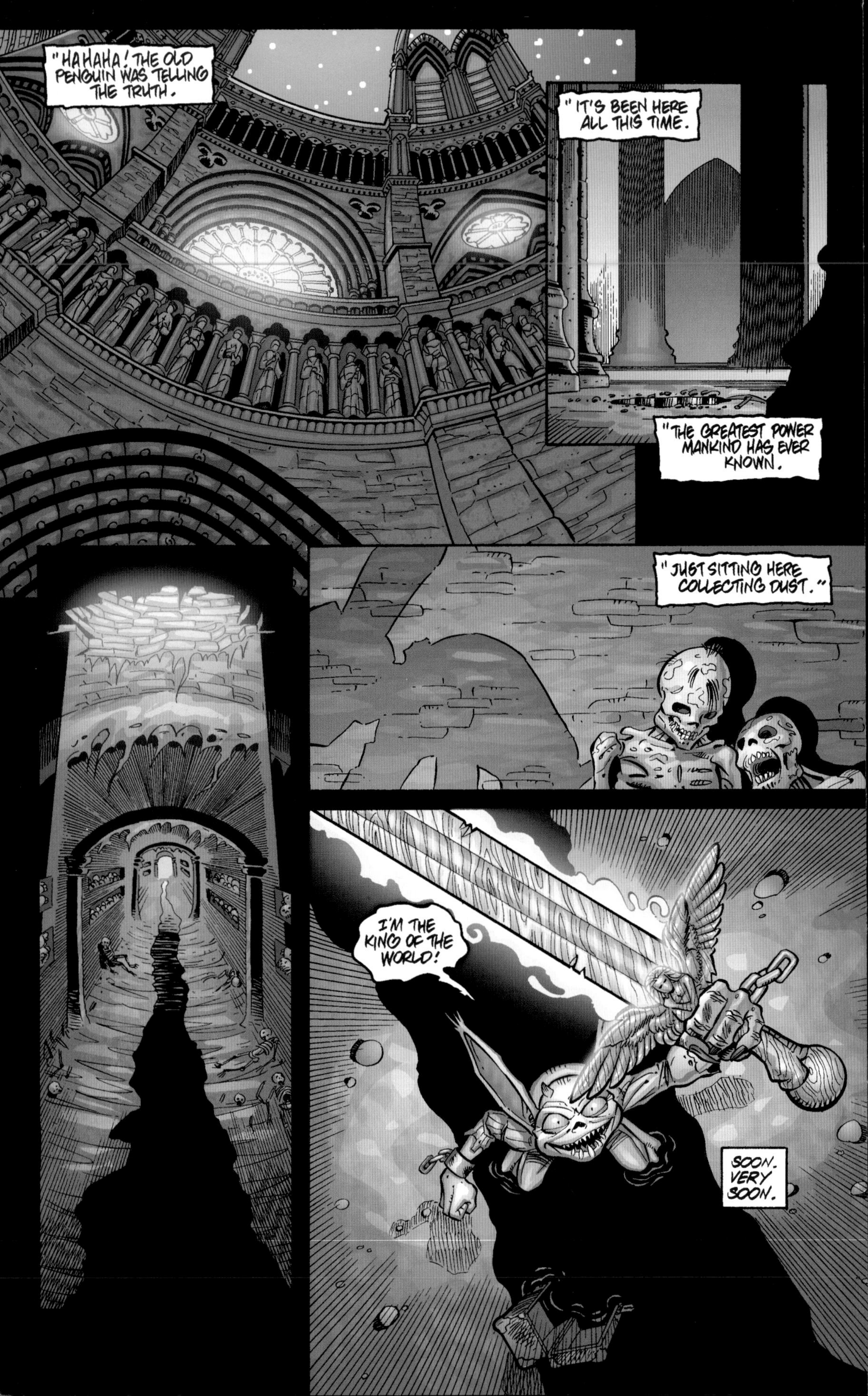
"HAHAHA! THE OLD PENGUIN WAS TELLING THE TRUTH.
"IT'S BEEN HERE ALL THIS TIME.
"THE GREATEST POWER MANKIND HAS EVER KNOWN.
"JUST SITTING HERE COLLECTING DUST."
I'M THE KING OF THE WORLD!
SOON. VERY SOON.

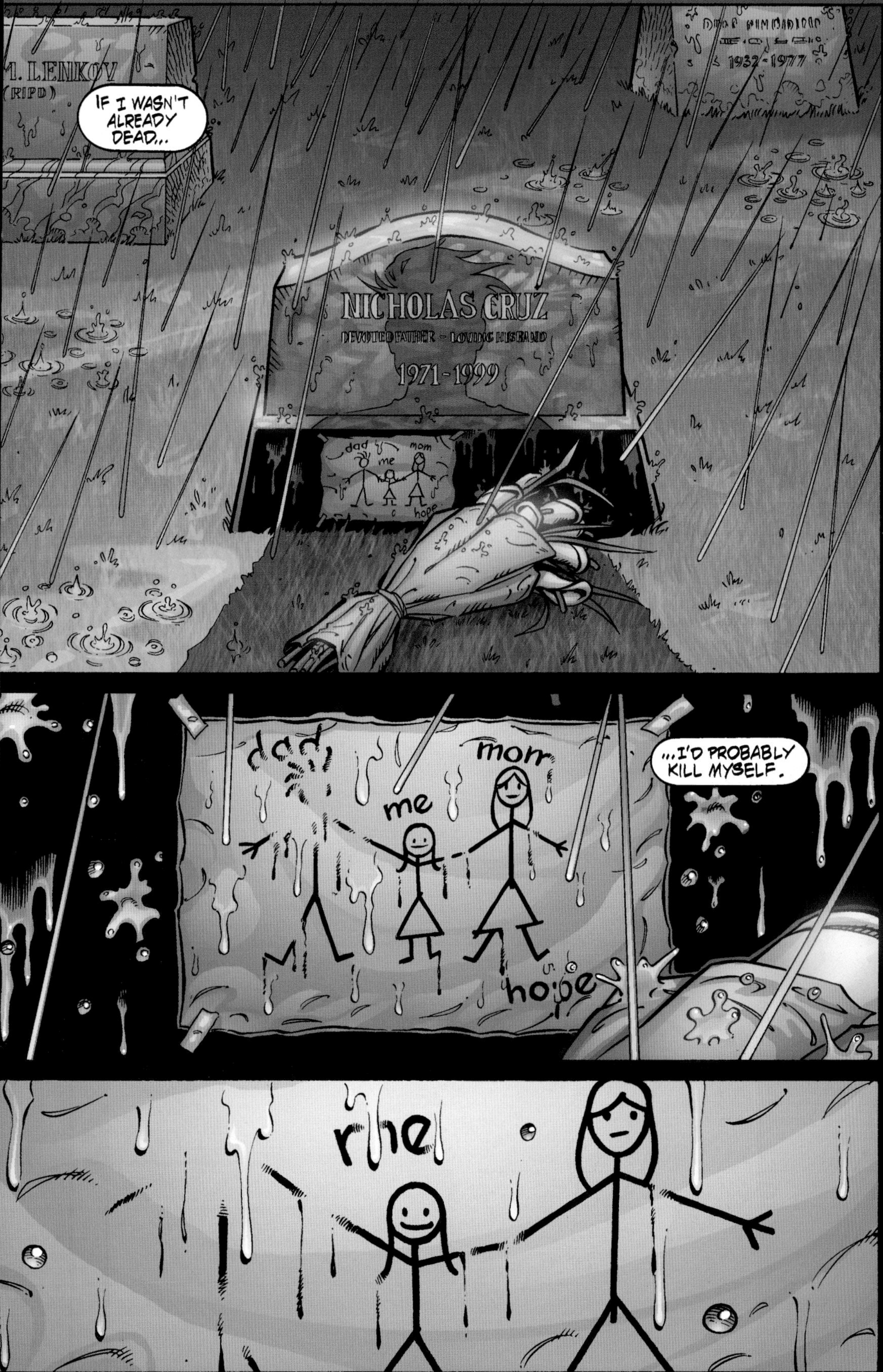
M. LENKOV
(RIPD)
1932-1977
IF I WASN'T ALREADY DEAD...
NICHOLAS CRUZ
DEVOTED FATHER – LOVING HUSBAND
1971-1999
dad
me
mom
hope
...I'D PROBABLY KILL MYSELF.

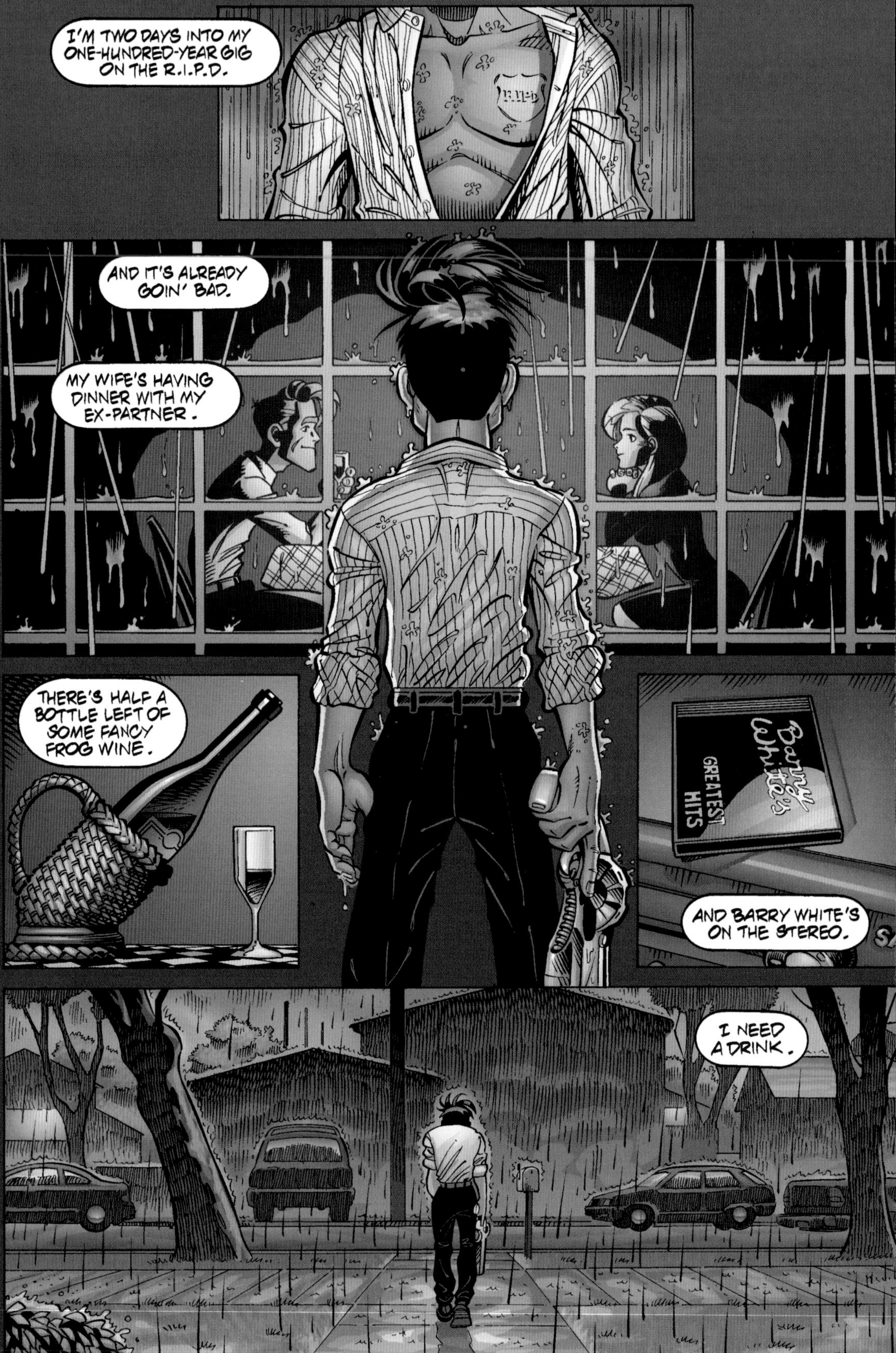
I'M TWO DAYS INTO MY ONE-HUNDRED-YEAR GIG ON THE R.I.P.D.
R.I.P.D.
AND IT'S ALREADY GOIN' BAD.
MY WIFE'S HAVING DINNER WITH MY EX-PARTNER.
THERE'S HALF A BOTTLE LEFT OF SOME FANCY FROG WINE.
Barry White's GREATEST HITS
AND BARRY WHITE'S ON THE STEREO.
I NEED A DRINK.

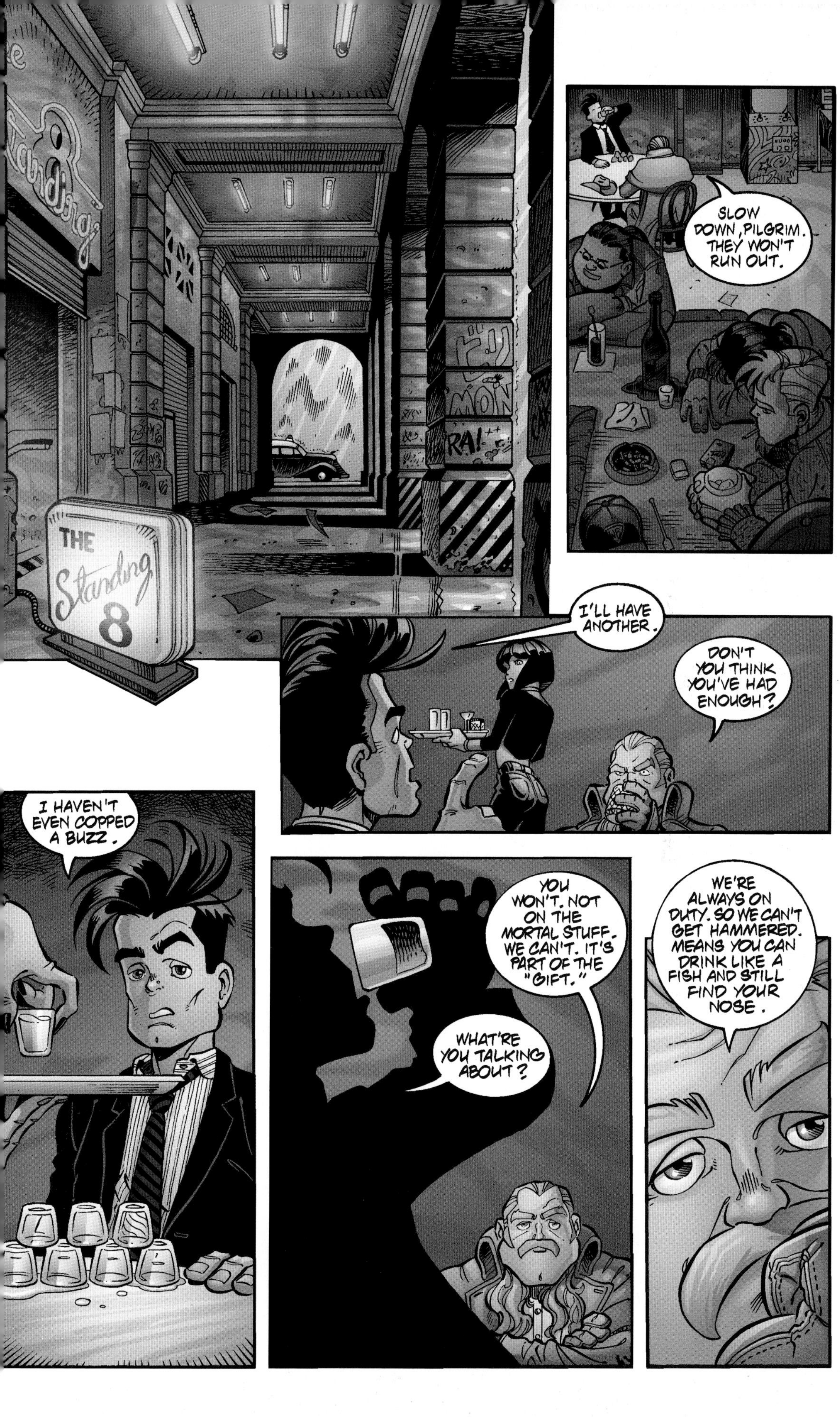
THE Standing 8
SLOW DOWN, PILGRIM. THEY WON'T RUN OUT.
I'LL HAVE ANOTHER.
DON'T YOU THINK YOU'VE HAD ENOUGH?
I HAVEN'T EVEN COPPED A BUZZ.
YOU WON'T. NOT ON THE MORTAL STUFF. WE CAN'T. IT'S PART OF THE "GIFT."
WHAT'RE YOU TALKING ABOUT?
WE'RE ALWAYS ON DUTY. SO WE CAN'T GET HAMMERED. MEANS YOU CAN DRINK LIKE A FISH AND STILL FIND YOUR NOSE.

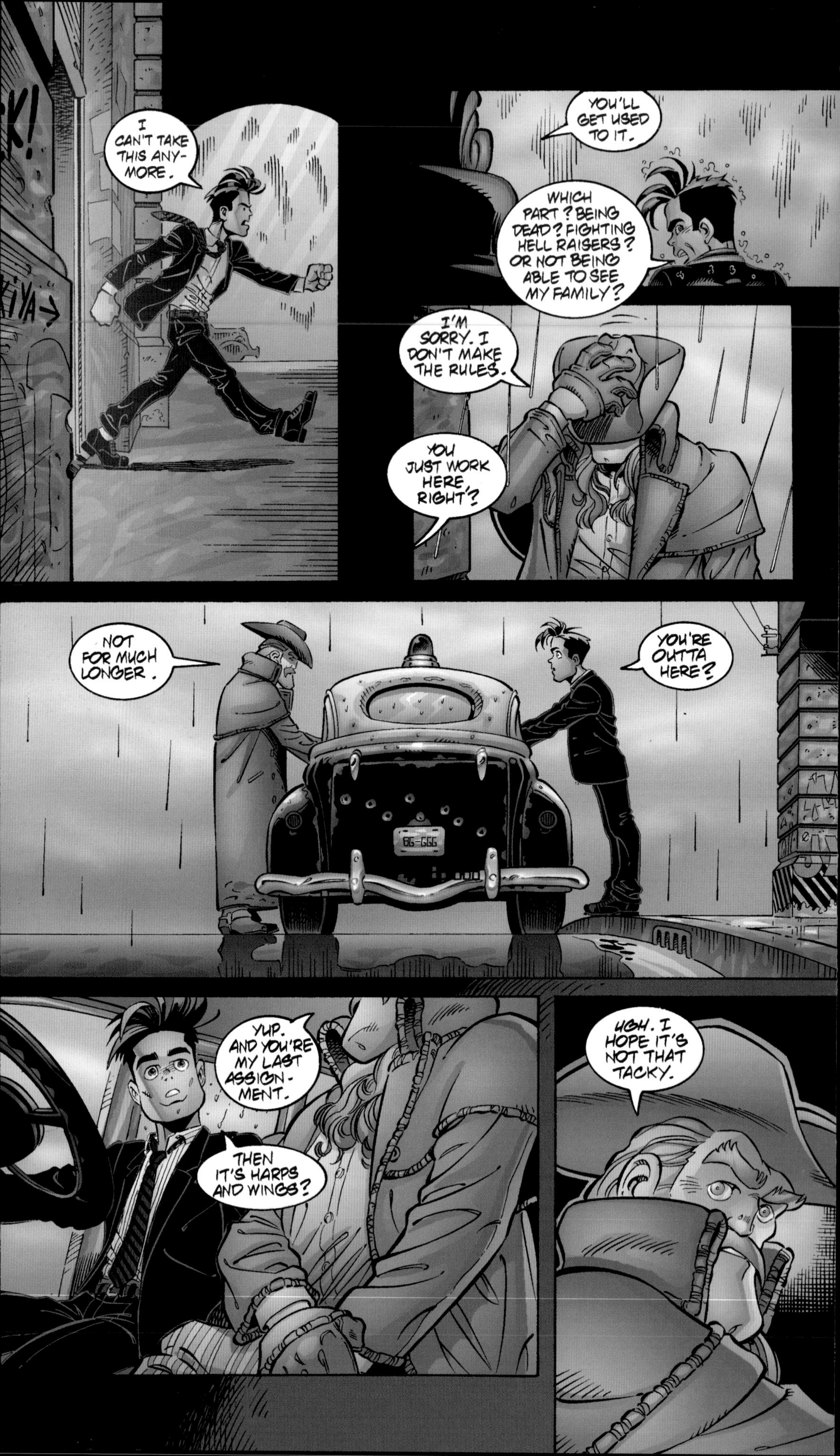
I CAN'T TAKE THIS ANYMORE.
YOU'LL GET USED TO IT.
WHICH PART? BEING DEAD? FIGHTING HELL RAISERS? OR NOT BEING ABLE TO SEE MY FAMILY?
I'M SORRY. I DON'T MAKE THE RULES.
YOU JUST WORK HERE RIGHT?
NOT FOR MUCH LONGER.
YOU'RE OUTTA HERE?
BG-GGG
YUP. AND YOU'RE MY LAST ASSIGNMENT.
THEN IT'S HARPS AND WINGS?
UGH. I HOPE IT'S NOT THAT TACKY.

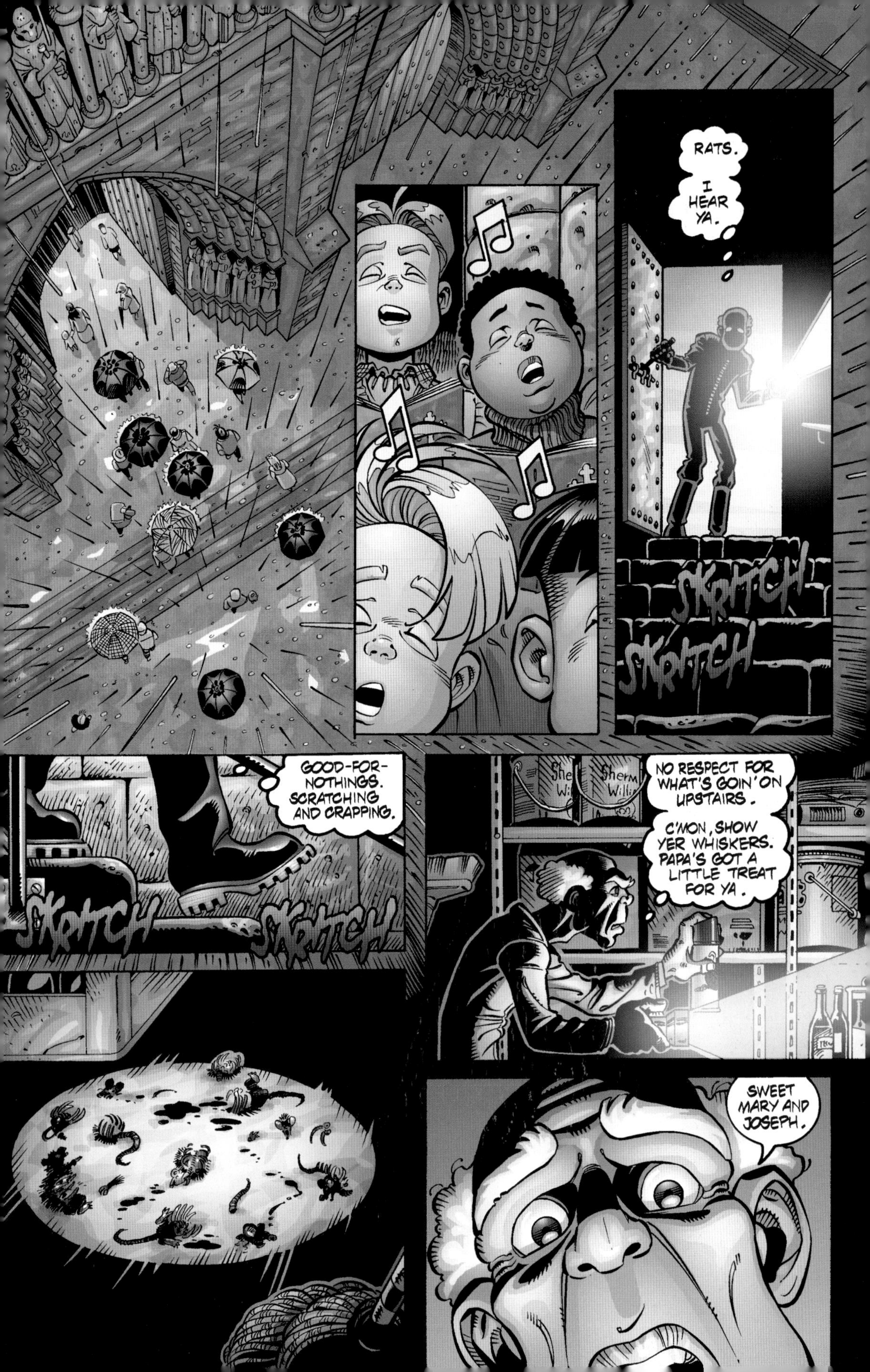
RATS.
I HEAR YA.
SKRITCH
SKRITCH
GOOD-FOR-NOTHINGS. SCRATCHING AND CRAPPING.
SKRITCH
SKRITCH
NO RESPECT FOR WHAT'S GOIN' ON UPSTAIRS.
C'MON, SHOW YER WHISKERS. PAPA'S GOT A LITTLE TREAT FOR YA.
SWEET MARY AND JOSEPH.

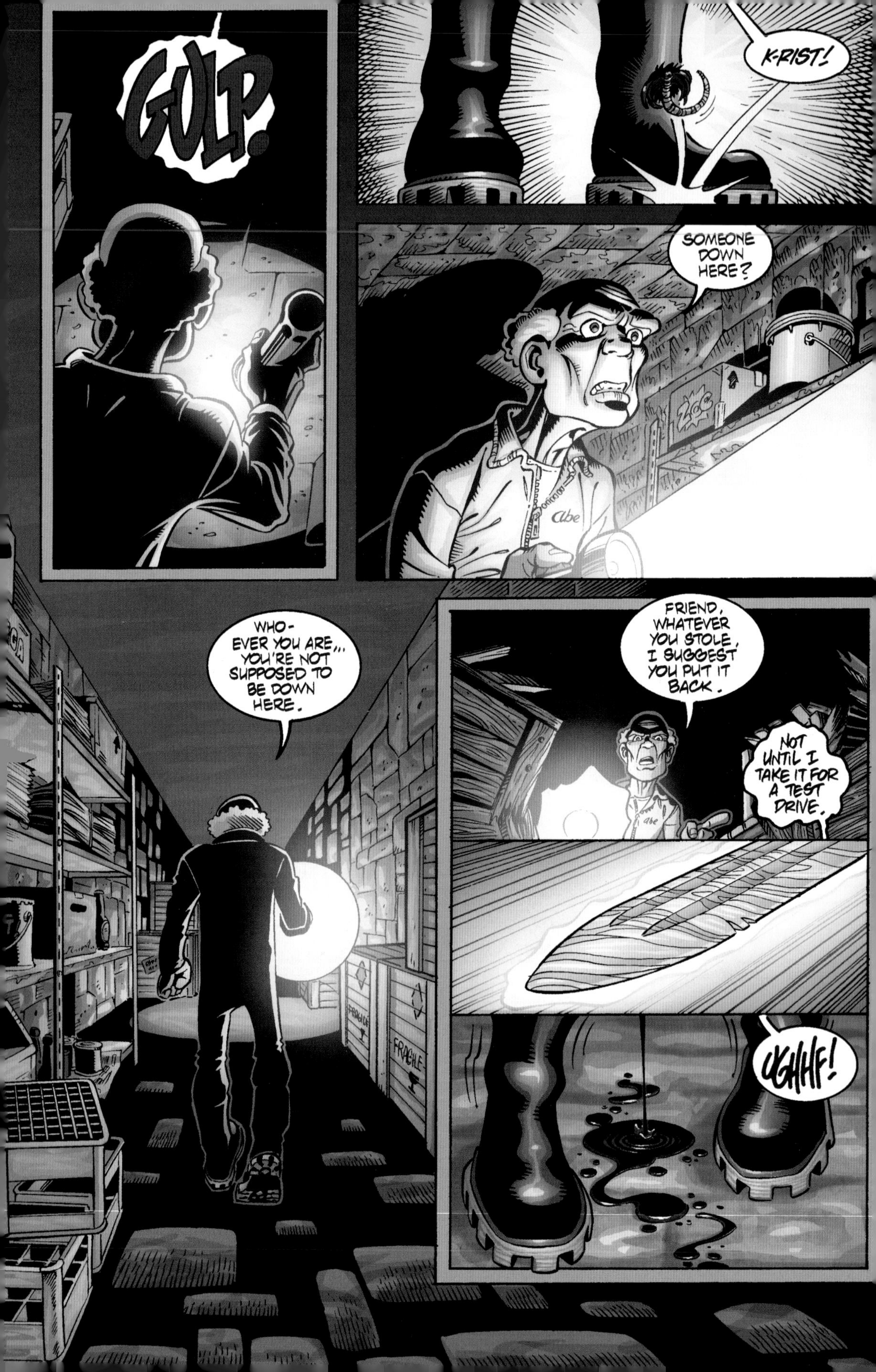
GULP!
K-RIST!
SOMEONE DOWN HERE?
WHO-EVER YOU ARE,,, YOU'RE NOT SUPPOSED TO BE DOWN HERE.
FRIEND, WHATEVER YOU STOLE, I SUGGEST YOU PUT IT BACK.
NOT UNTIL I TAKE IT FOR A TEST DRIVE.
UGHHF!

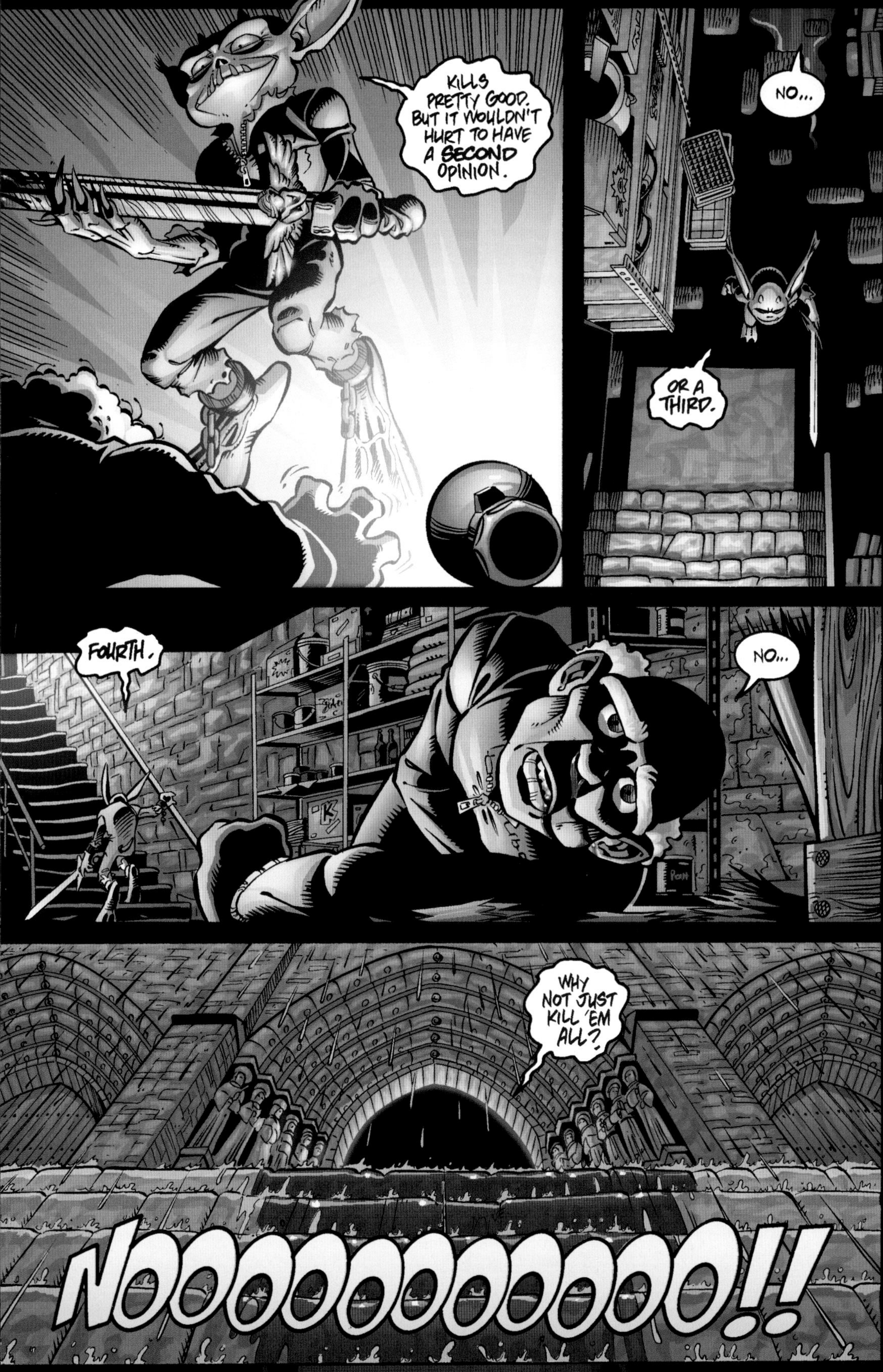
KILLS PRETTY GOOD. BUT IT WOULDN'T HURT TO HAVE A SECOND OPINION.
NO...
OR A THIRD.
FOURTH.
NO...
WHY NOT JUST KILL 'EM ALL?
NOOOOOOOOOOOO!!

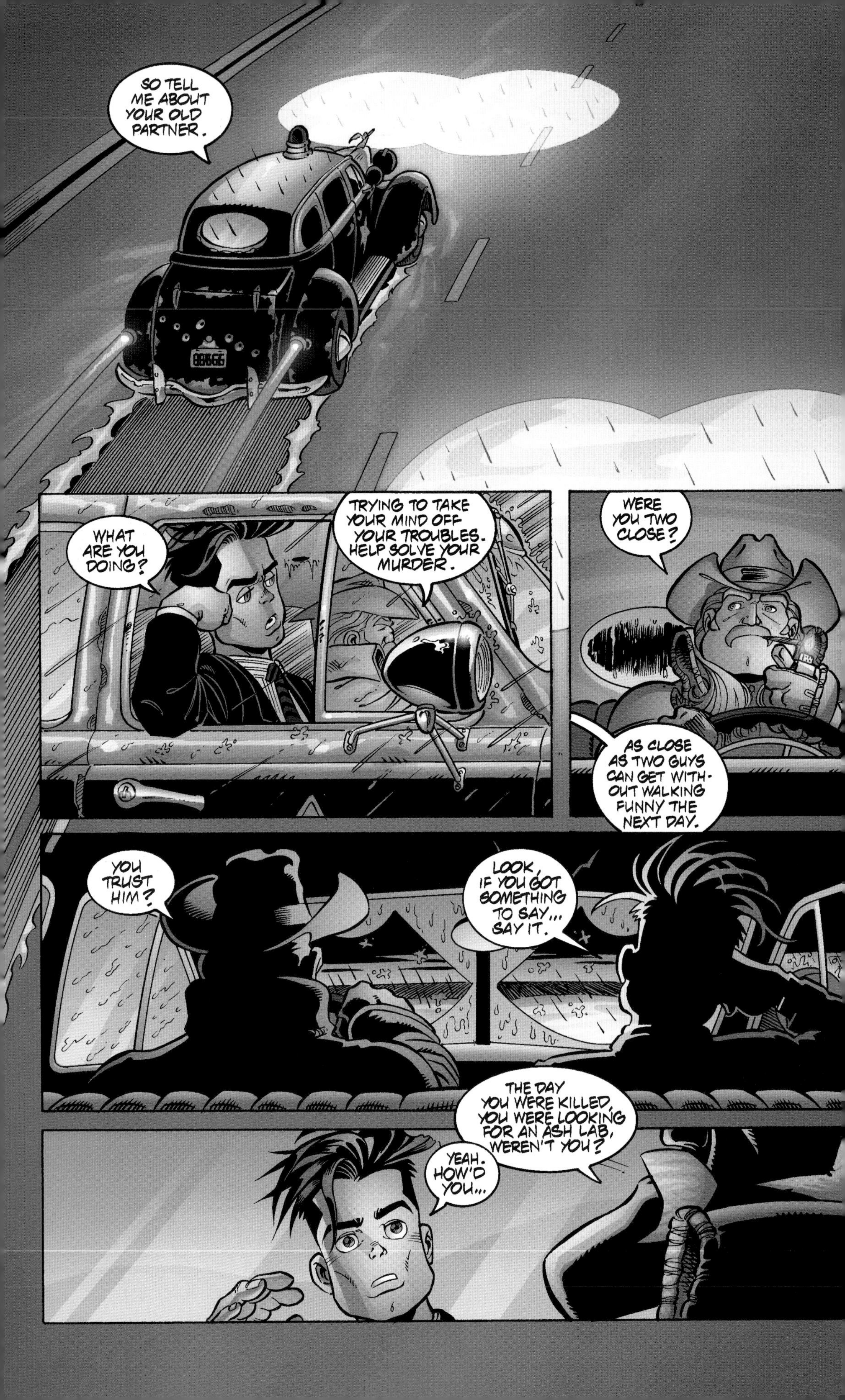
SO TELL ME ABOUT YOUR OLD PARTNER.
WHAT ARE YOU DOING?
TRYING TO TAKE YOUR MIND OFF YOUR TROUBLES. HELP SOLVE YOUR MURDER.
WERE YOU TWO CLOSE?
AS CLOSE AS TWO GUYS CAN GET WITH-OUT WALKING FUNNY THE NEXT DAY.
YOU TRUST HIM?
LOOK, IF YOU GOT SOMETHING TO SAY... SAY IT.
THE DAY YOU WERE KILLED, YOU WERE LOOKING FOR AN ASH LAB, WEREN'T YOU?
YEAH. HOW'D YOU...

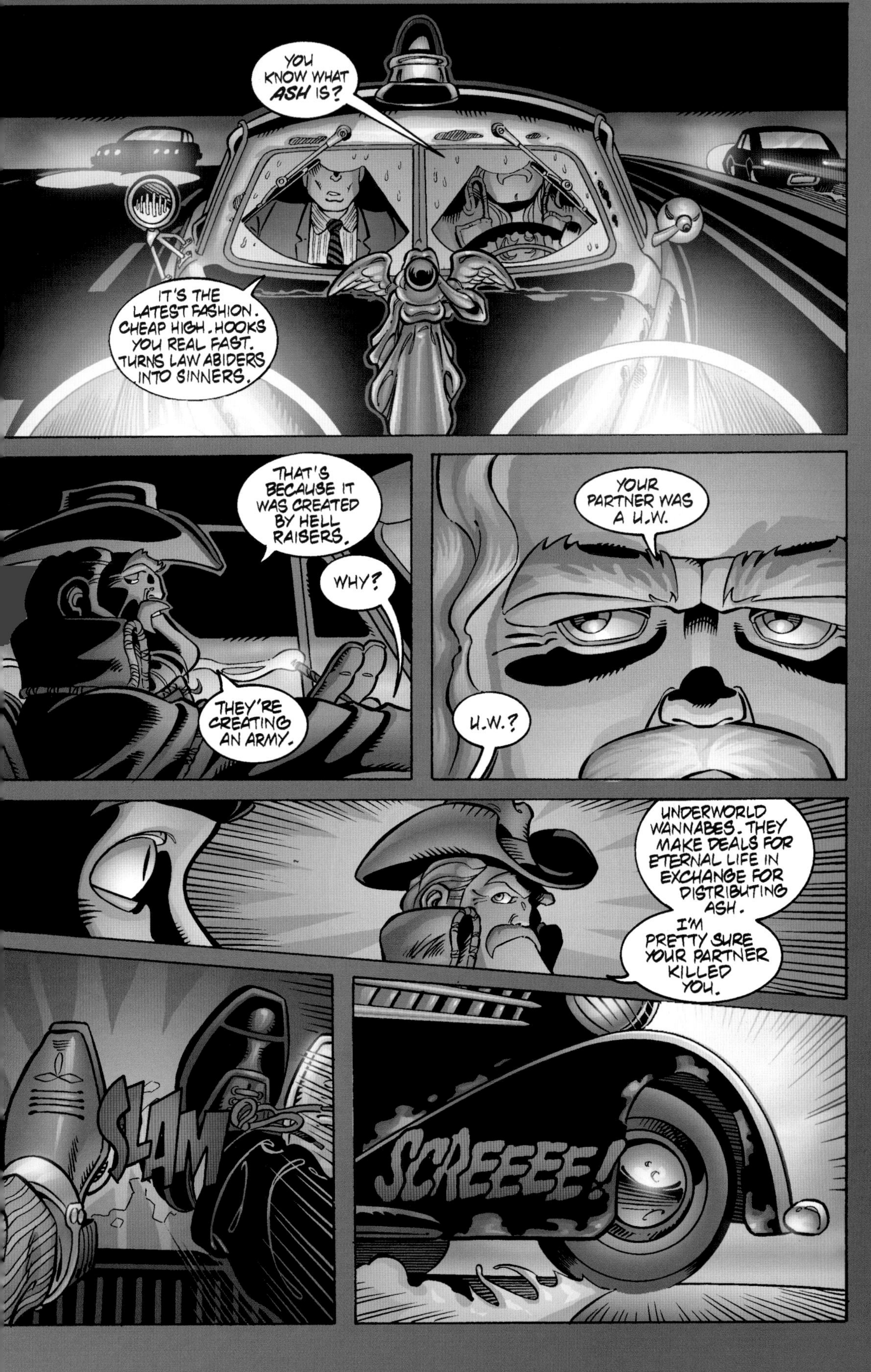
YOU KNOW WHAT ASH IS?
IT'S THE LATEST FASHION. CHEAP HIGH. HOOKS YOU REAL FAST. TURNS LAW ABIDERS INTO SINNERS.
THAT'S BECAUSE IT WAS CREATED BY HELL RAISERS.
WHY?
THEY'RE CREATING AN ARMY.
YOUR PARTNER WAS A U.W.
U.W.?
UNDERWORLD WANNABES. THEY MAKE DEALS FOR ETERNAL LIFE IN EXCHANGE FOR DISTRIBUTING ASH.
I'M PRETTY SURE YOUR PARTNER KILLED YOU.
SLAM
SCREEEEE!

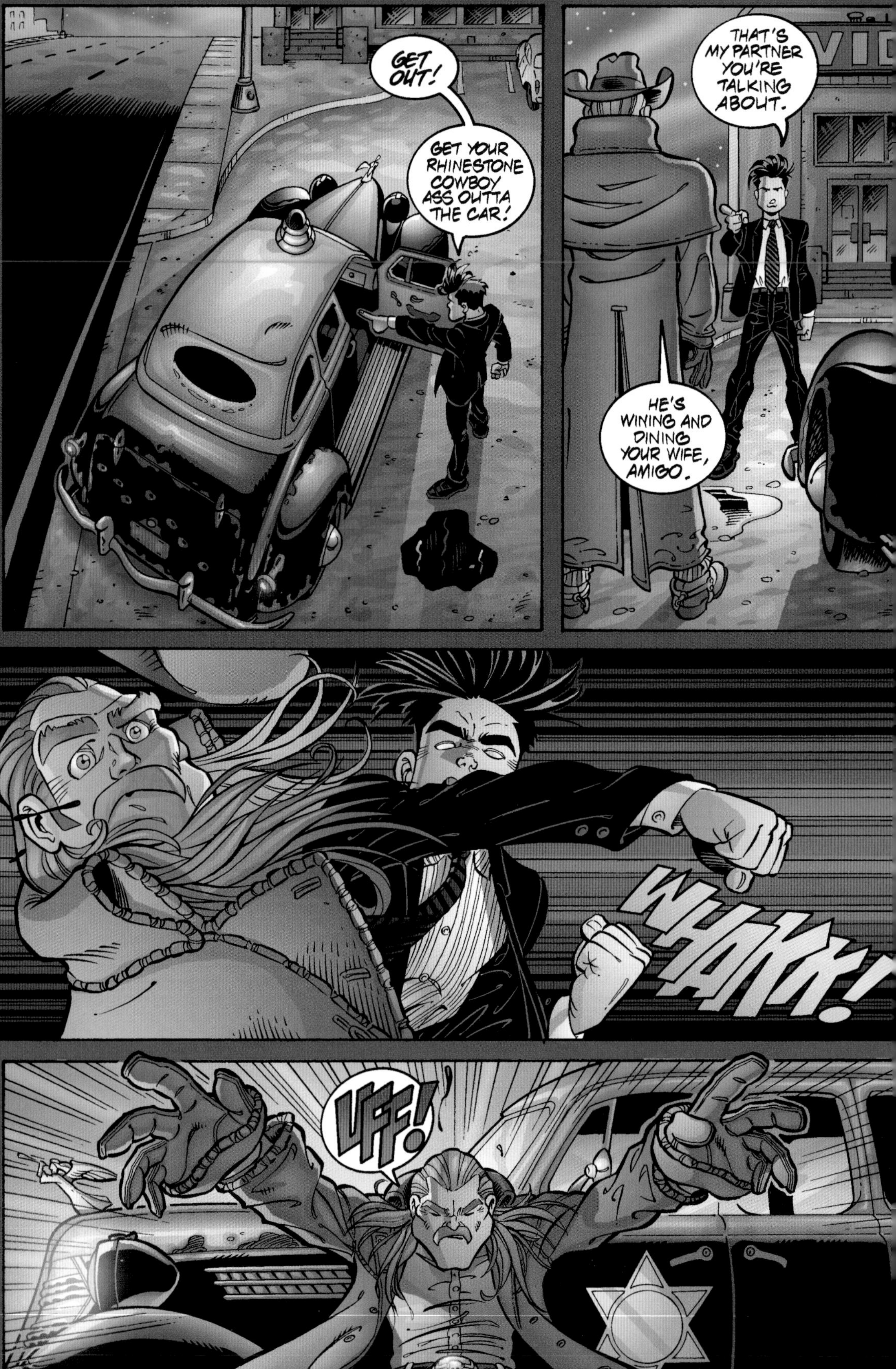
GET OUT!
GET YOUR RHINESTONE COWBOY ASS OUTTA THE CAR!
THAT'S MY PARTNER YOU'RE TALKING ABOUT.
HE'S WINING AND DINING YOUR WIFE, AMIGO.
WHAKK!
UFF!

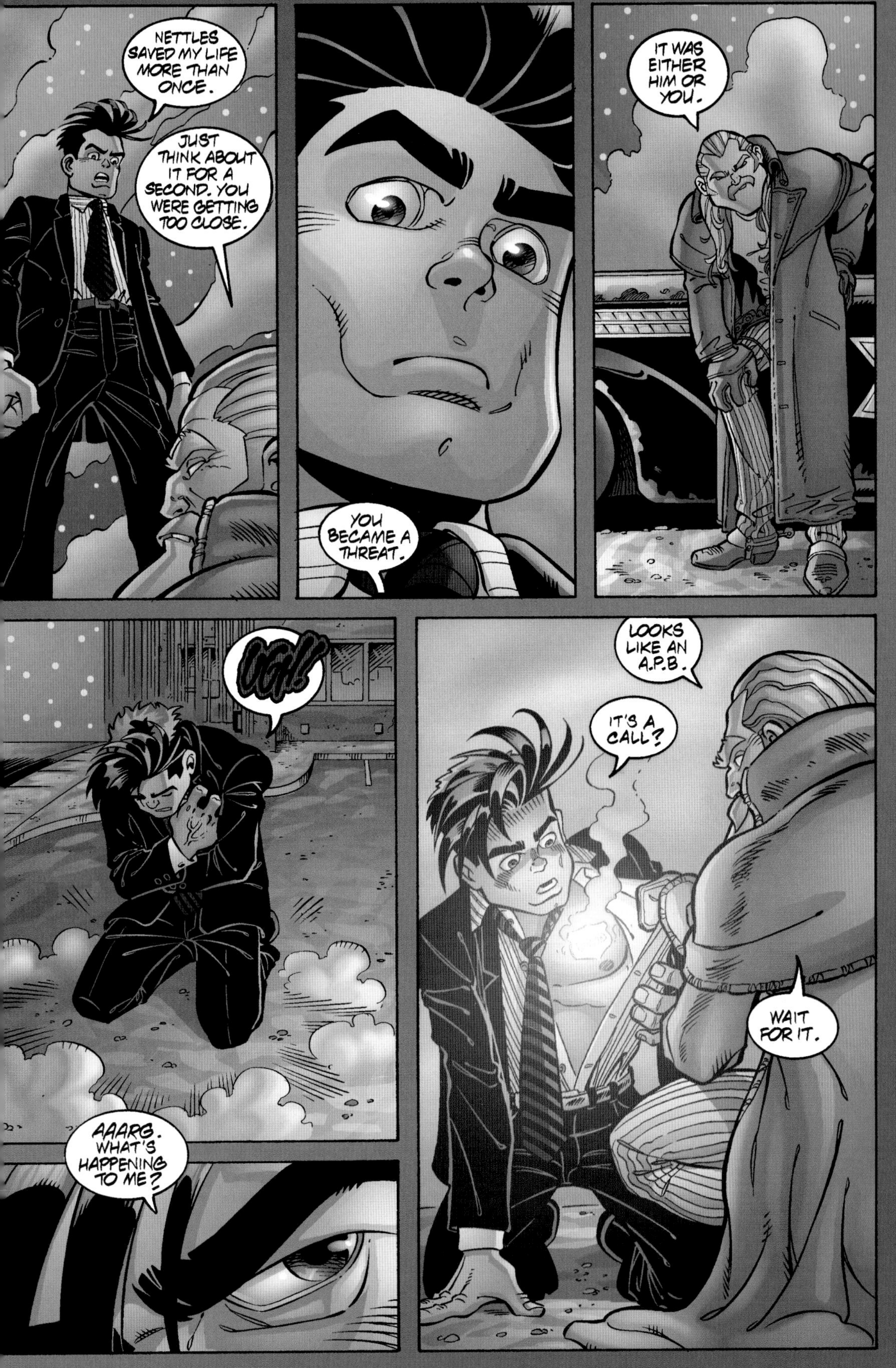
NETTLES SAVED MY LIFE MORE THAN ONCE.
JUST THINK ABOUT IT FOR A SECOND. YOU WERE GETTING TOO CLOSE.
YOU BECAME A THREAT.
IT WAS EITHER HIM OR YOU.
UGH!
AAARG. WHAT'S HAPPENING TO ME?
LOOKS LIKE AN A.P.B.
IT'S A CALL?
WAIT FOR IT.

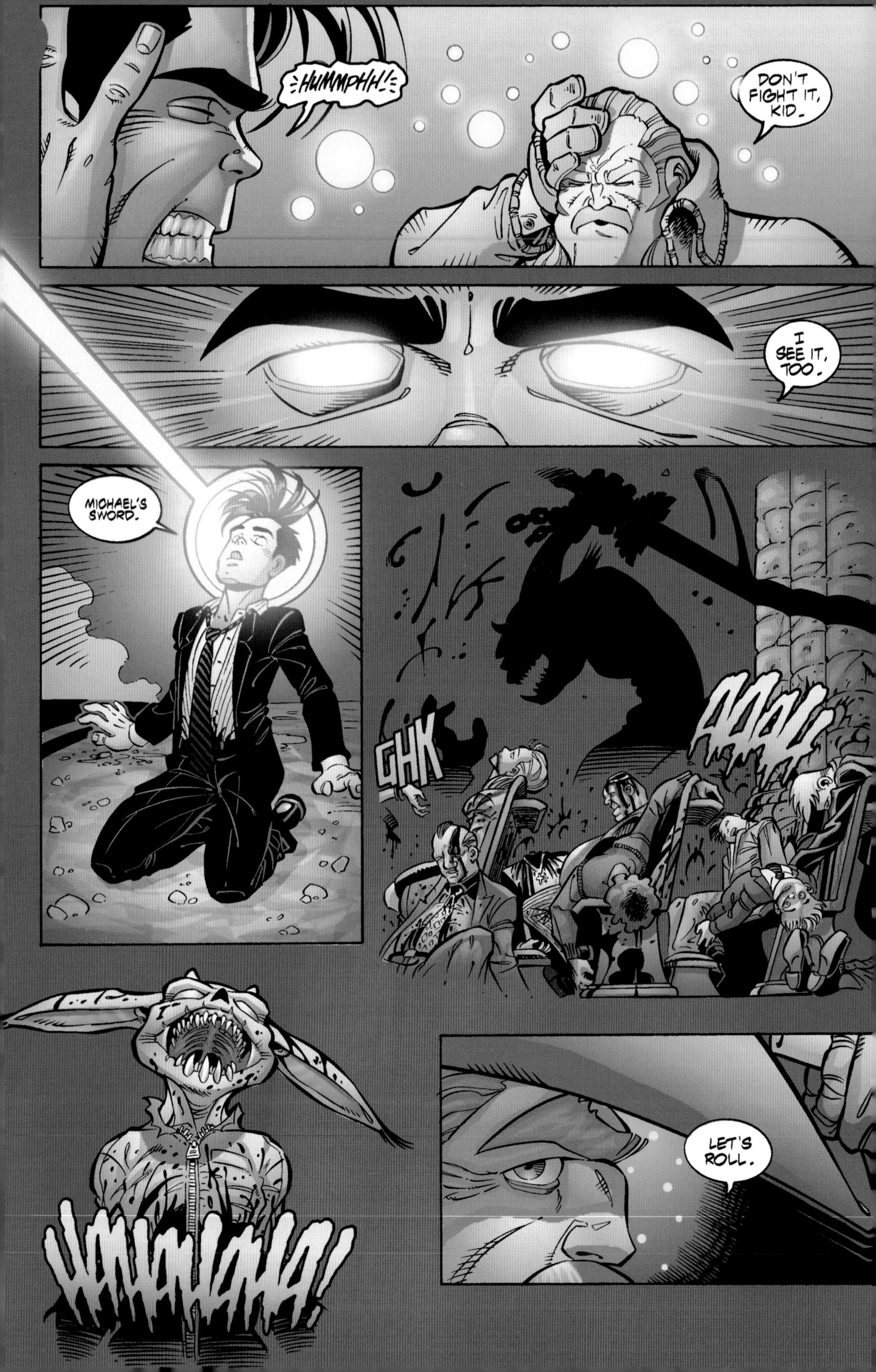
HUMMPHH!
DON'T FIGHT IT, KID.
I SEE IT, TOO.
MICHAEL'S SWORD.
GHK
AAAH
LET'S ROLL.
HAHAHA!

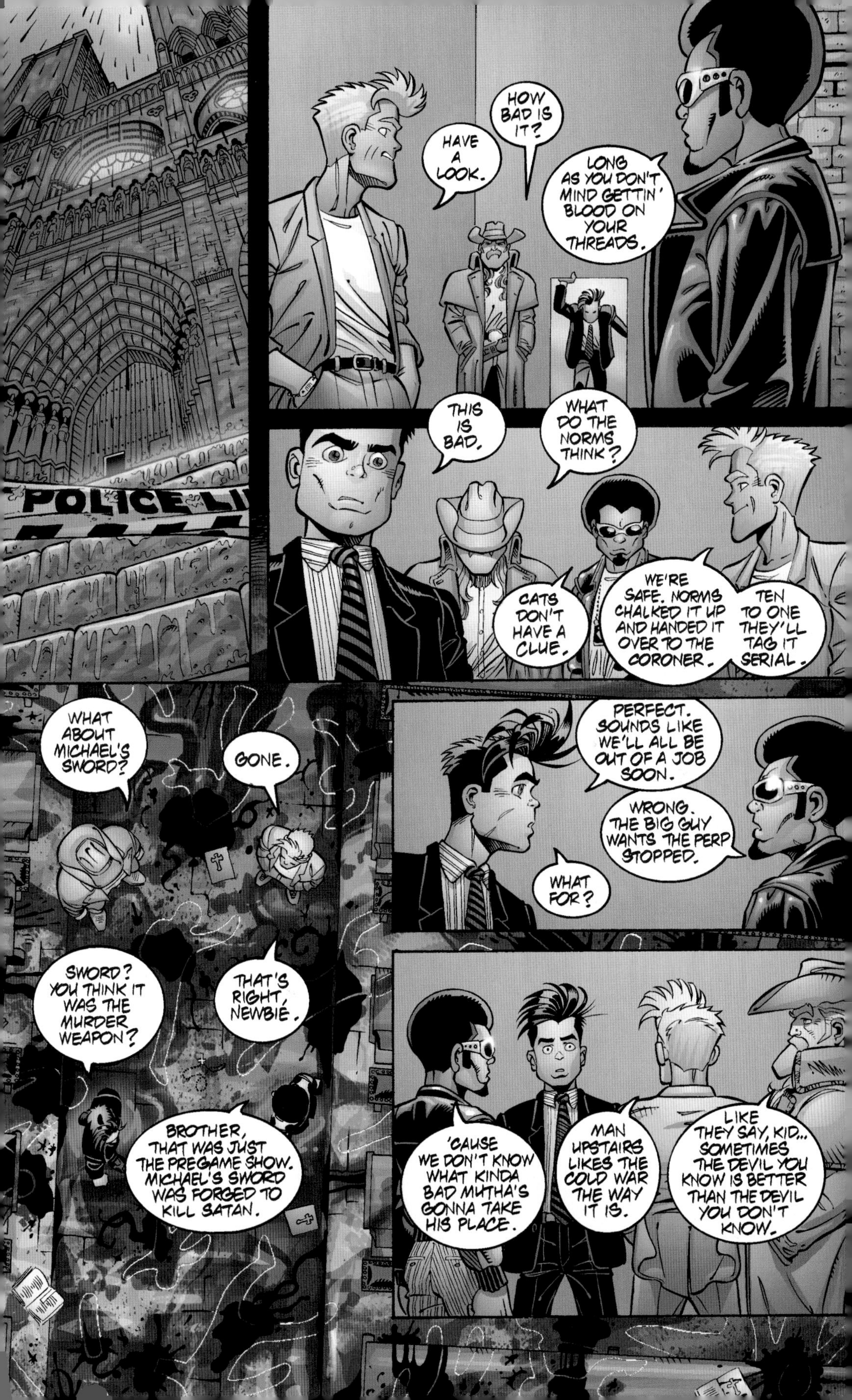
POLICE LI
HOW BAD IS IT?
HAVE A LOOK.
LONG AS YOU DON'T MIND GETTIN' BLOOD ON YOUR THREADS.
THIS IS BAD.
WHAT DO THE NORMS THINK?
CATS DON'T HAVE A CLUE.
WE'RE SAFE. NORMS CHALKED IT UP AND HANDED IT OVER TO THE CORONER.
TEN TO ONE THEY'LL TAG IT SERIAL.
WHAT ABOUT MICHAEL'S SWORD?
GONE.
SWORD? YOU THINK IT WAS THE MURDER WEAPON?
THAT'S RIGHT, NEWBIE.
BROTHER, THAT WAS JUST THE PREGAME SHOW. MICHAEL'S SWORD WAS FORGED TO KILL SATAN.
PERFECT. SOUNDS LIKE WE'LL ALL BE OUT OF A JOB SOON.
WRONG. THE BIG GUY WANTS THE PERP STOPPED.
WHAT FOR?
'CAUSE WE DON'T KNOW WHAT KINDA BAD MUTHA'S GONNA TAKE HIS PLACE.
MAN UPSTAIRS LIKES THE COLD WAR THE WAY IT IS.
LIKE THEY SAY, KID... SOMETIMES THE DEVIL YOU KNOW IS BETTER THAN THE DEVIL YOU DON'T KNOW.

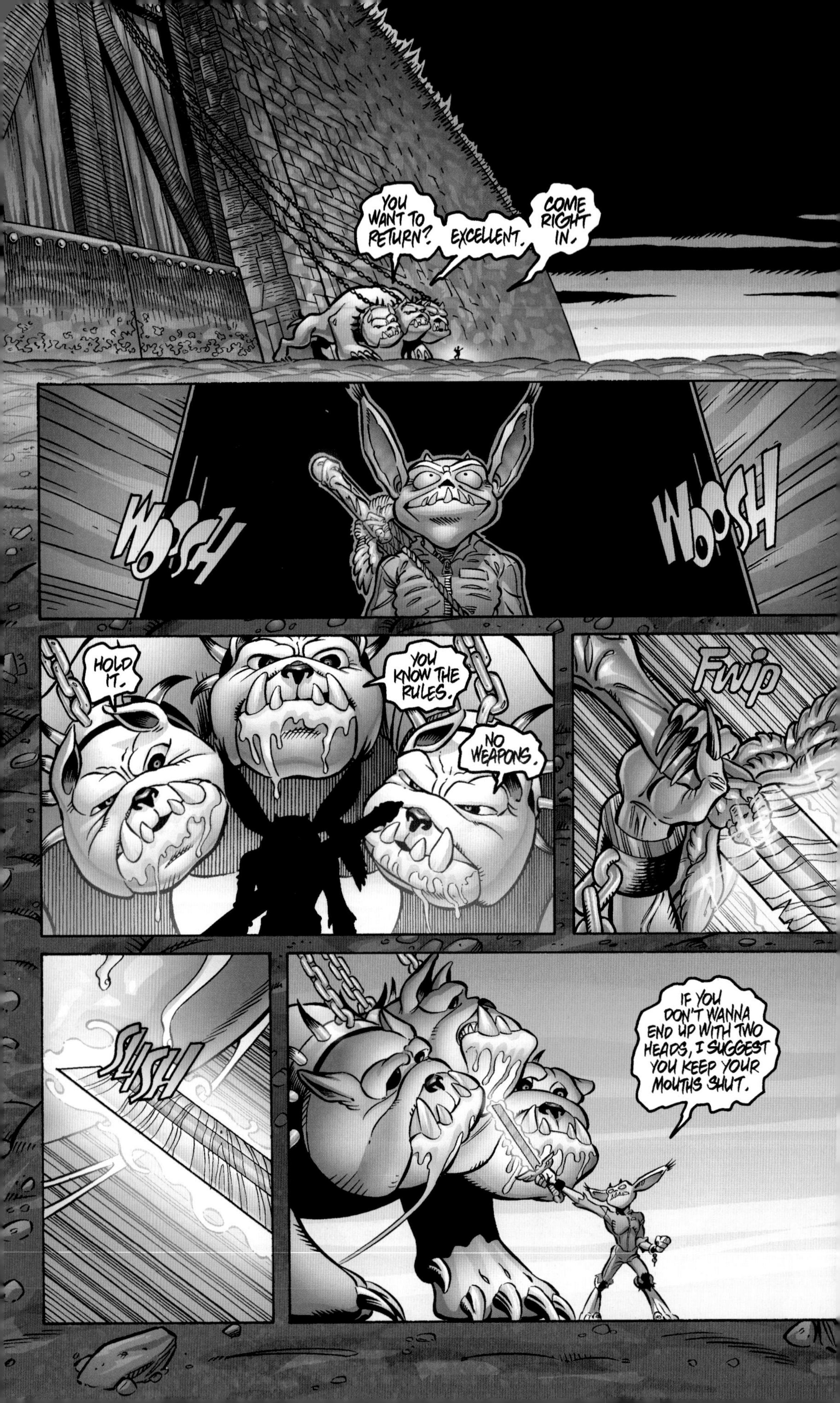

YOU WANT TO RETURN?
EXCELLENT.
COME RIGHT IN.
WOOSH
WOOSH
HOLD IT.
YOU KNOW THE RULES.
NO WEAPONS.
Fwip
SLISH
IF YOU DON'T WANNA END UP WITH TWO HEADS, I SUGGEST YOU KEEP YOUR MOUTHS SHUT.

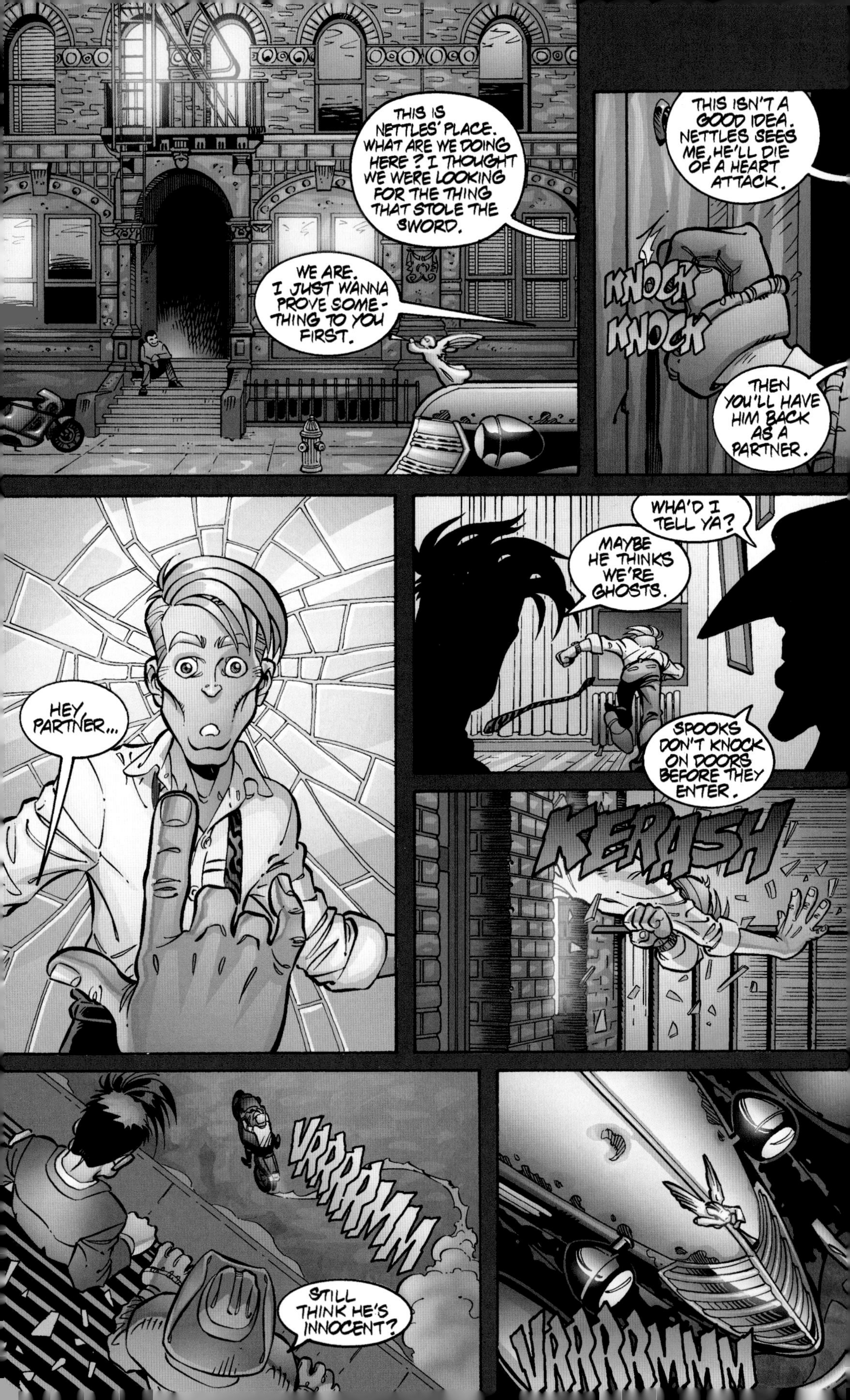

THIS IS NETTLES' PLACE. WHAT ARE WE DOING HERE? I THOUGHT WE WERE LOOKING FOR THE THING THAT STOLE THE SWORD.
WE ARE. I JUST WANNA PROVE SOME-THING TO YOU FIRST.
THIS ISN'T A GOOD IDEA. NETTLES SEES ME, HE'LL DIE OF A HEART ATTACK.
KNOCK KNOCK
THEN YOU'LL HAVE HIM BACK AS A PARTNER.
HEY PARTNER...
WHA'D I TELL YA?
MAYBE HE THINKS WE'RE GHOSTS.
SPOOKS DON'T KNOCK ON DOORS BEFORE THEY ENTER.
KERASH
VRRRRMM
STILL THINK HE'S INNOCENT?
VRRRRMMM

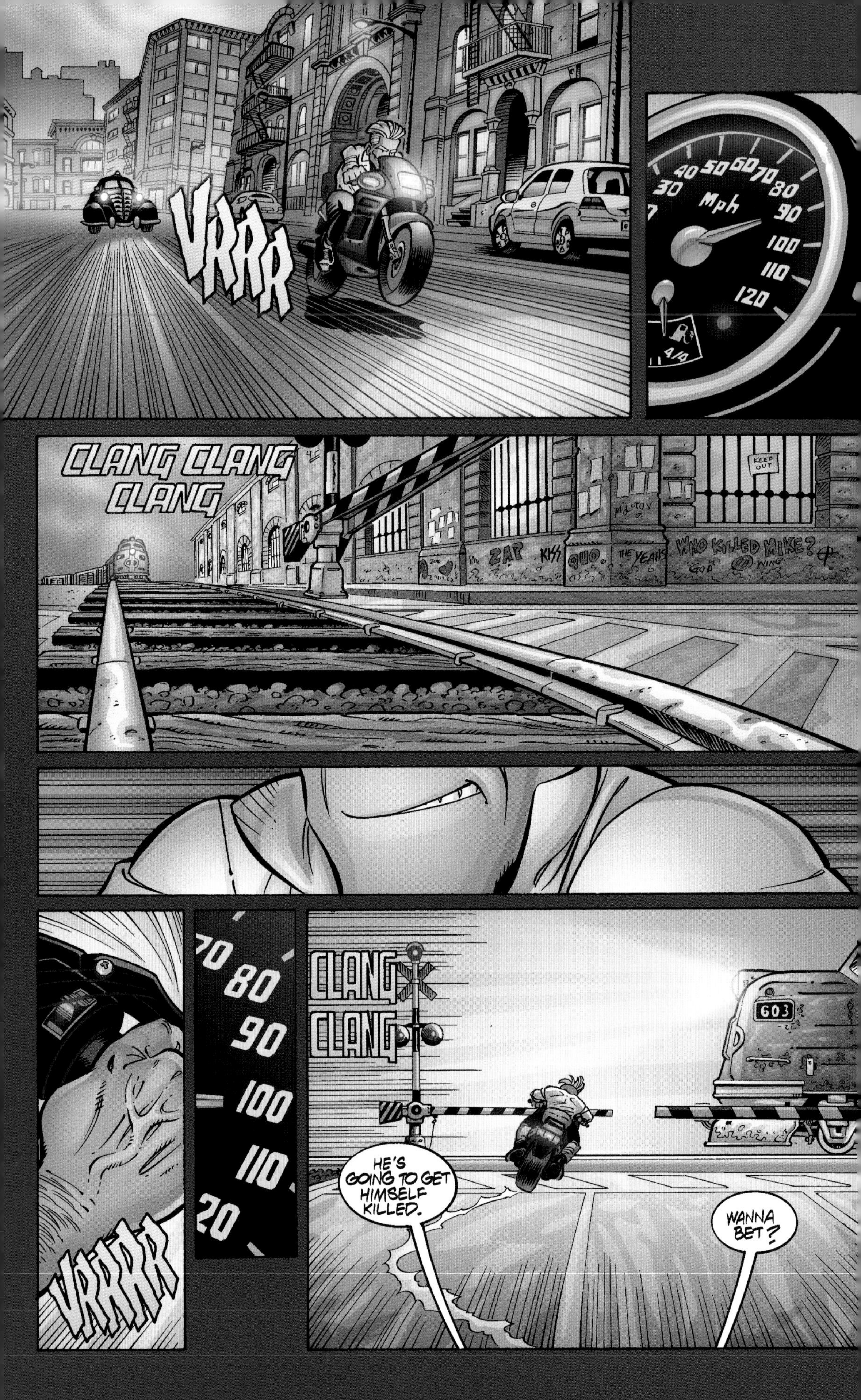
VRRR
Mph
CLANG CLANG CLANG
KEEP OUT
WHO KILLED MIKE?
ZAP
KISS
QUO
THE YEARS
CLANG CLANG
603
VRRRR
HE'S GOING TO GET HIMSELF KILLED.
WANNA BET?

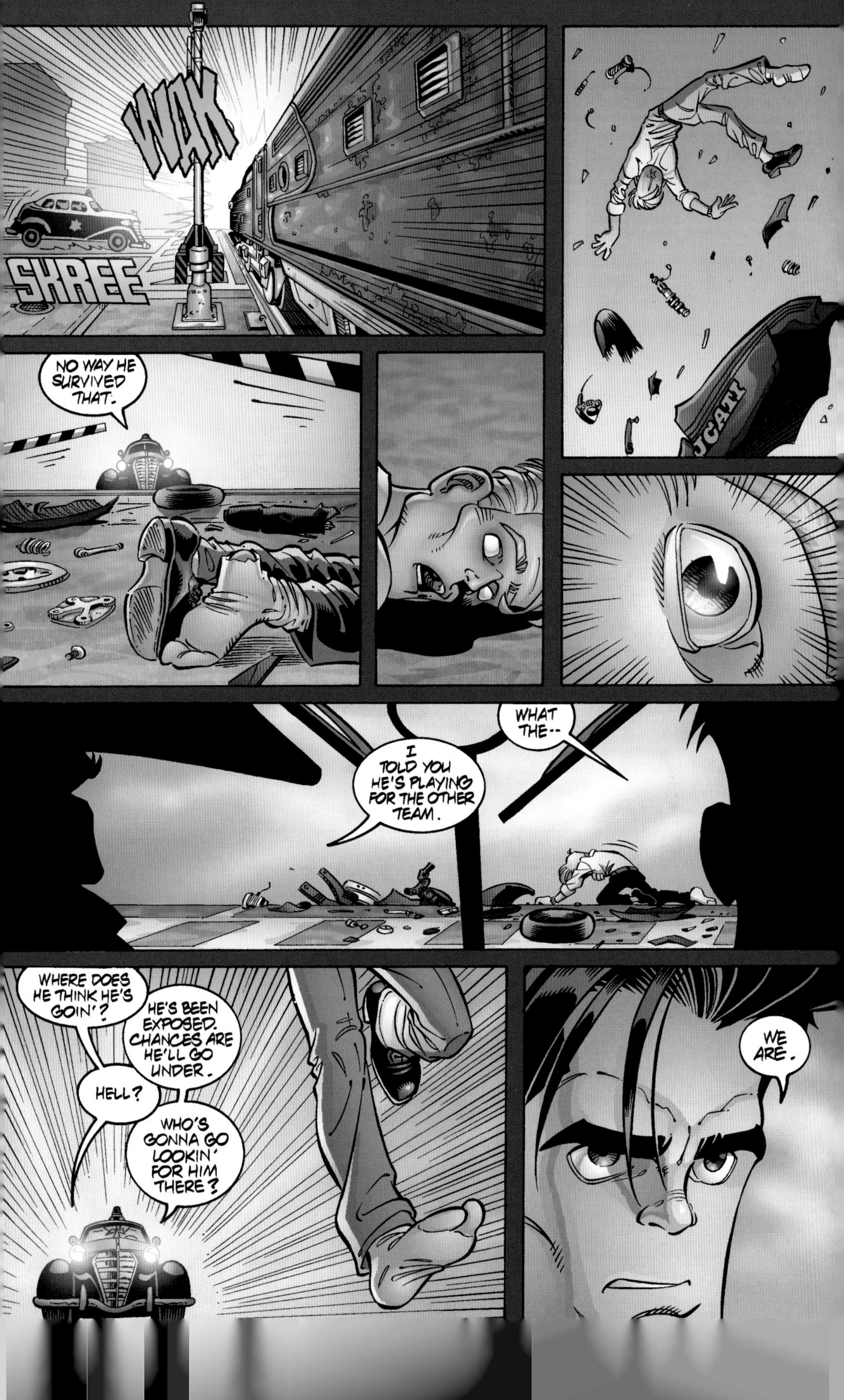
WOK
SKREE
NO WAY HE SURVIVED THAT.
WHAT THE--
I TOLD YOU HE'S PLAYING FOR THE OTHER TEAM.
WHERE DOES HE THINK HE'S GOIN'?
HE'S BEEN EXPOSED. CHANCES ARE HE'LL GO UNDER.
HELL?
WHO'S GONNA GO LOOKIN' FOR HIM THERE?
WE ARE.

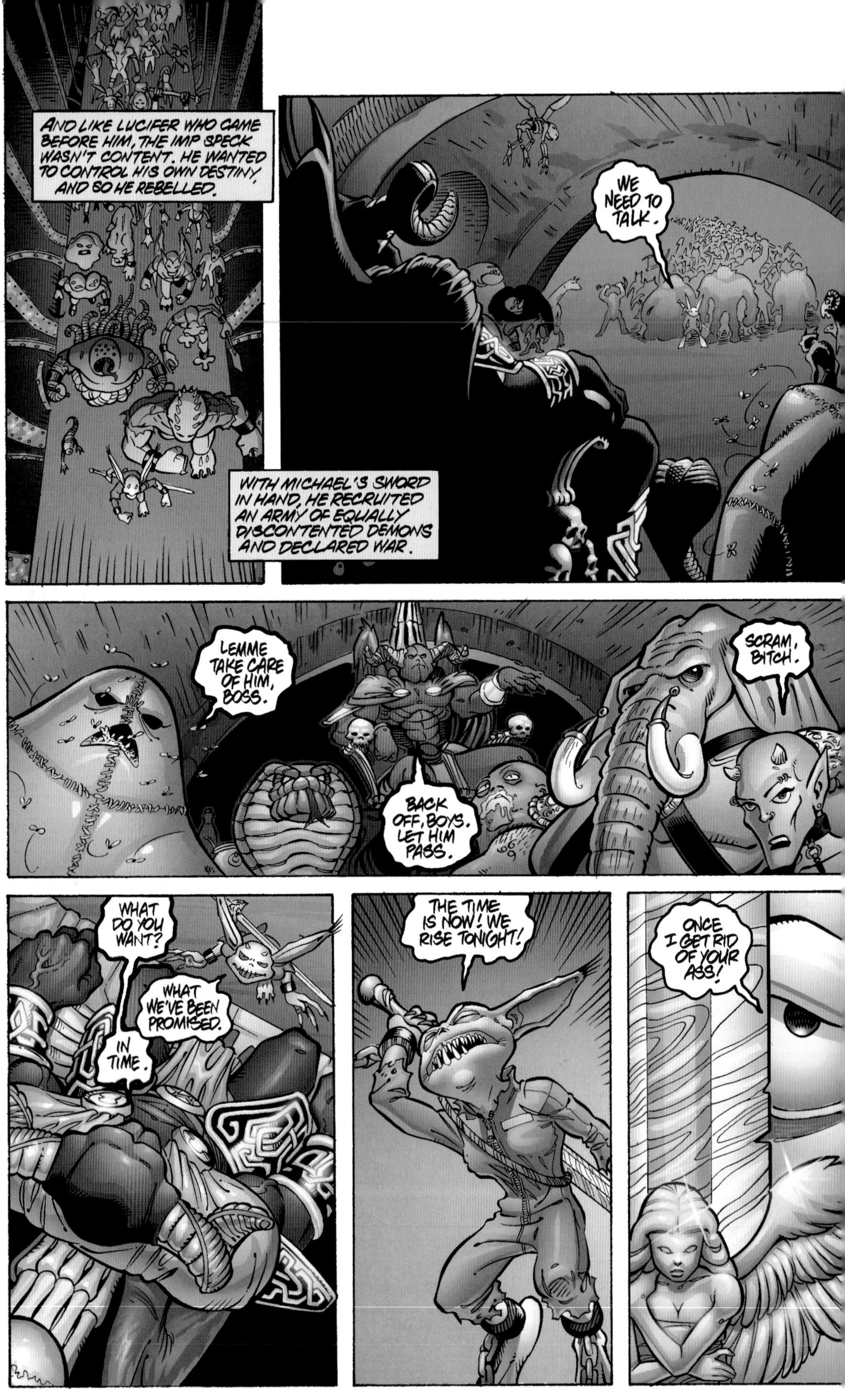
AND LIKE LUCIFER WHO CAME BEFORE HIM, THE IMP SPECK WASN'T CONTENT. HE WANTED TO CONTROL HIS OWN DESTINY, AND SO HE REBELLED.
WITH MICHAEL'S SWORD IN HAND, HE RECRUITED AN ARMY OF EQUALLY DISCONTENTED DEMONS AND DECLARED WAR.
WE NEED TO TALK.
LEMME TAKE CARE OF HIM, BOSS.
SCRAM, BITCH.
BACK OFF, BOYS. LET HIM PASS.
WHAT DO YOU WANT?
WHAT WE'VE BEEN PROMISED.
IN TIME.
THE TIME IS NOW! WE RISE TONIGHT!
ONCE I GET RID OF YOUR ASS!

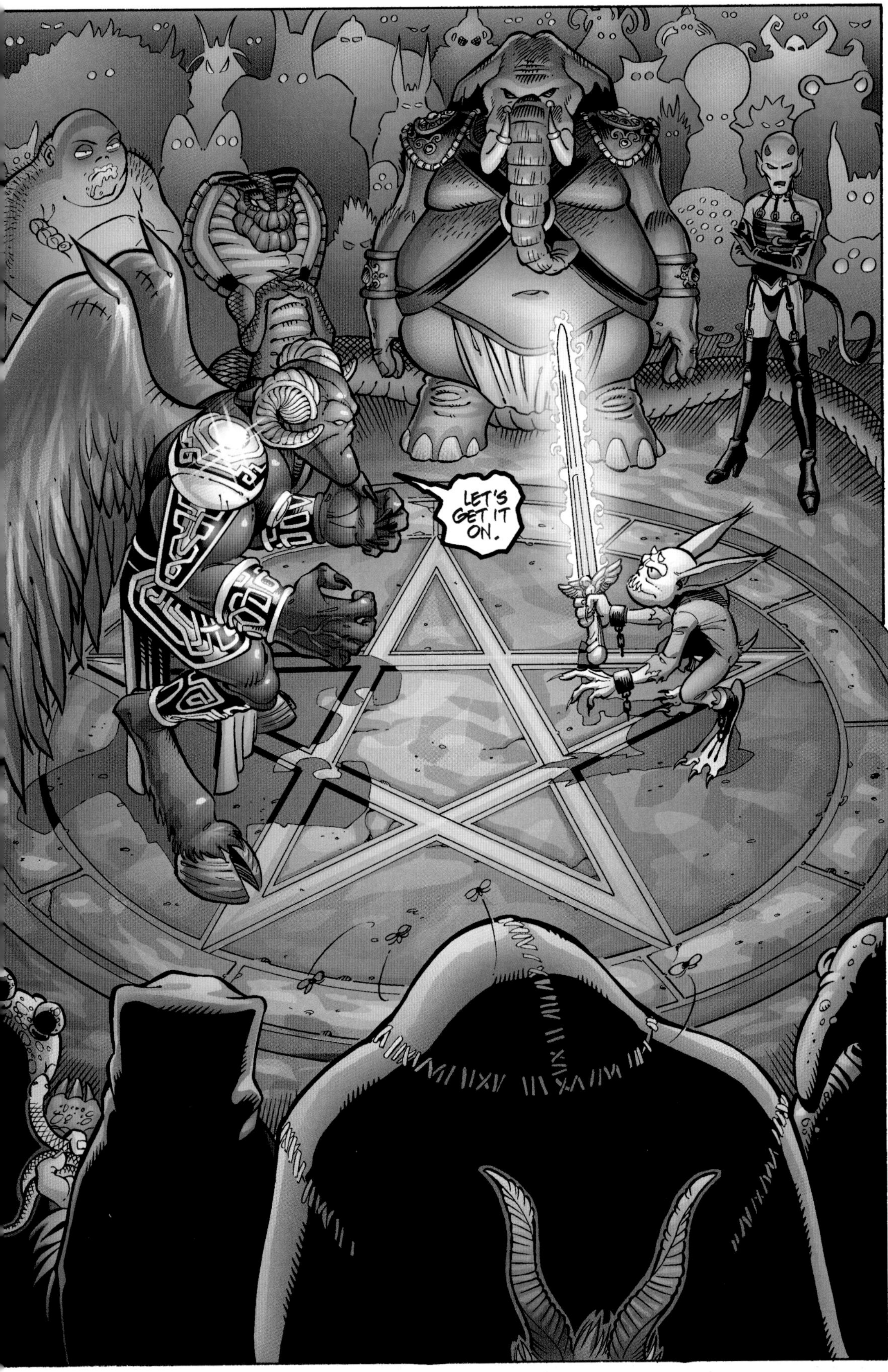
LET'S GET IT ON.

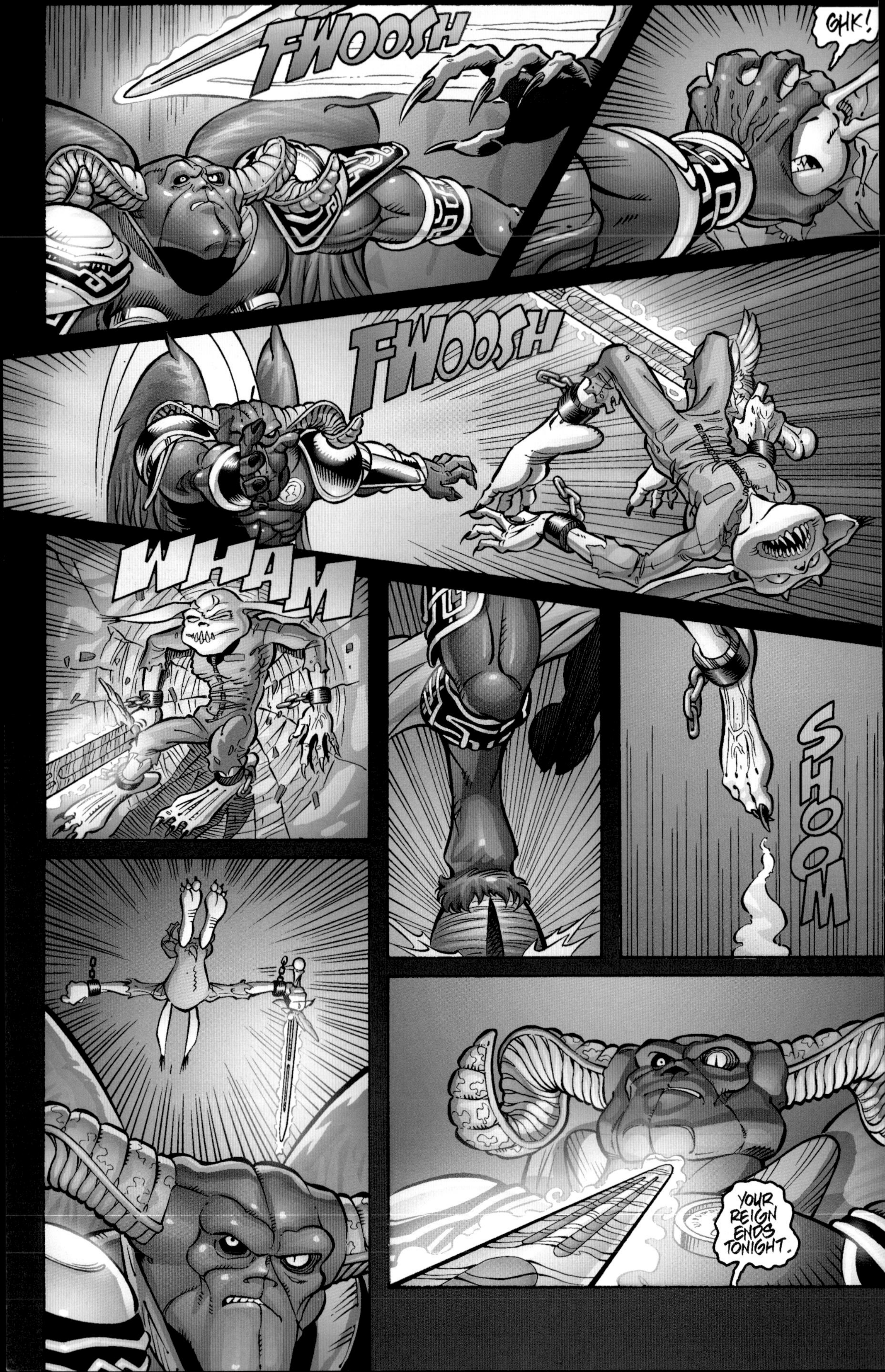
FWOOSH
GHK!
FWOOSH
WHAM
SHOOM
YOUR REIGN ENDS TONIGHT.

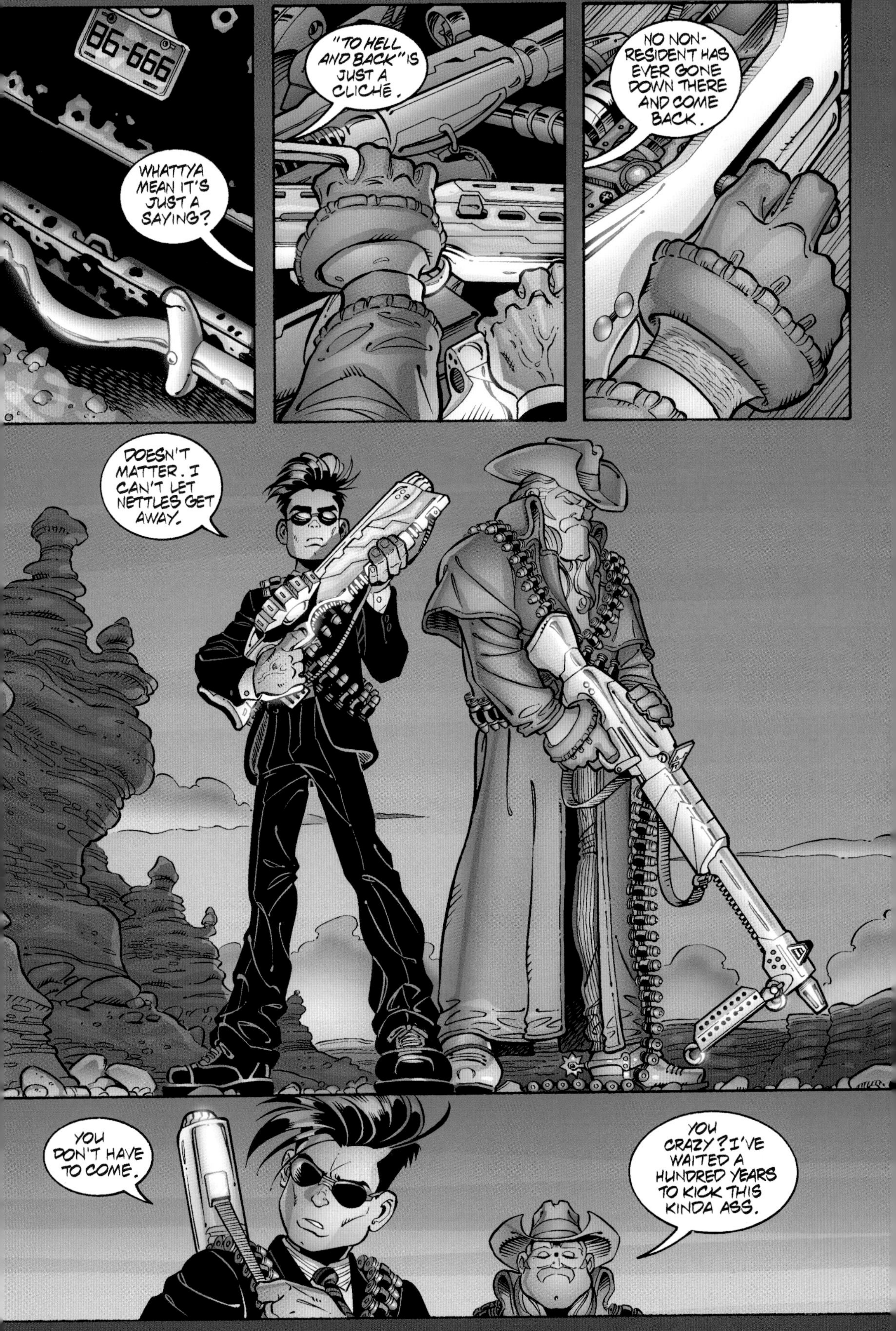

86-666
WHATTYA MEAN IT'S JUST A SAYING?
"TO HELL AND BACK" IS JUST A CLICHÉ.
NO NON-RESIDENT HAS EVER GONE DOWN THERE AND COME BACK.
DOESN'T MATTER. I CAN'T LET NETTLES GET AWAY.
YOU DON'T HAVE TO COME.
YOU CRAZY? I'VE WAITED A HUNDRED YEARS TO KICK THIS KINDA ASS.

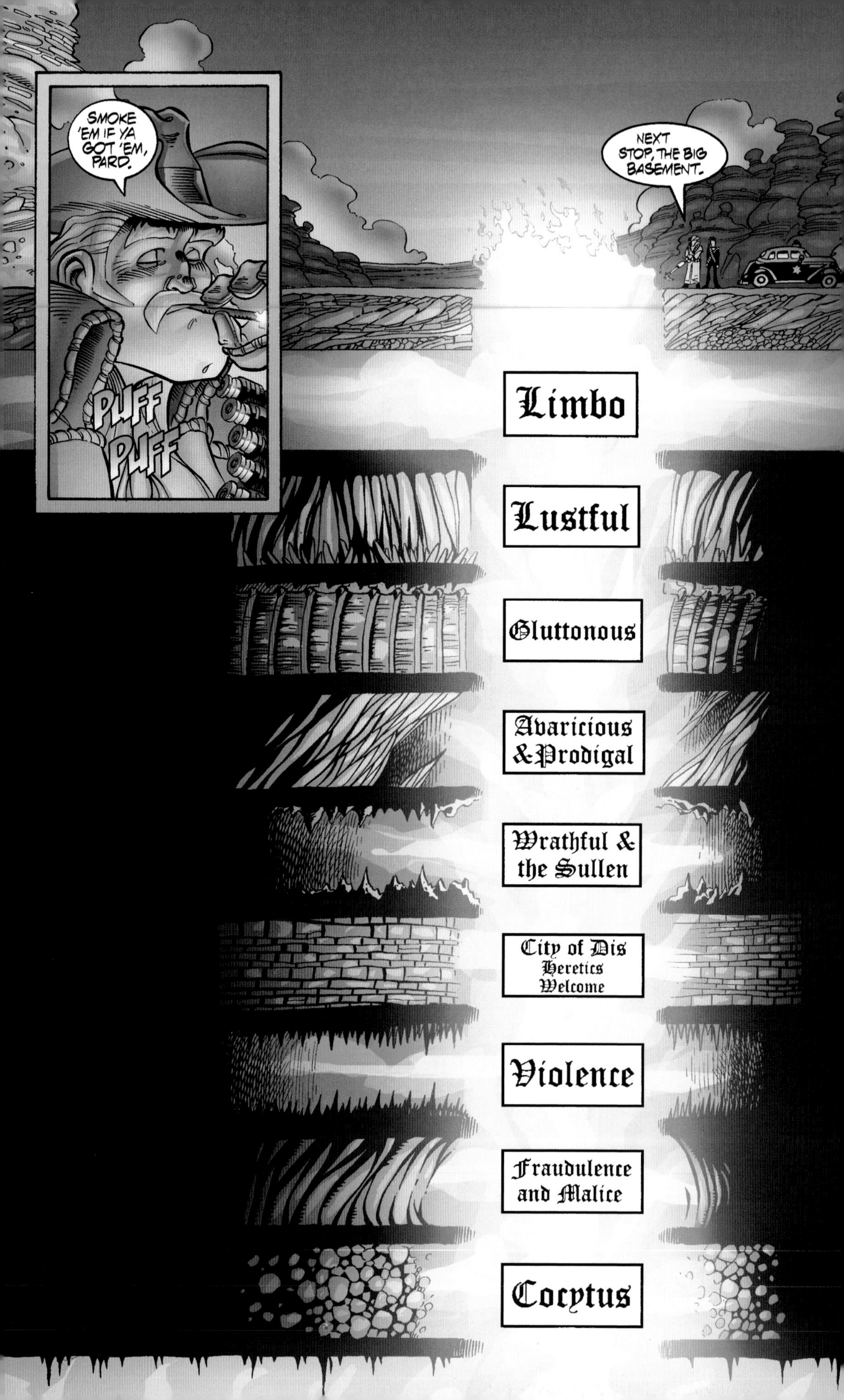
SMOKE 'EM IF YA GOT 'EM, PARD.
PUFF PUFF
NEXT STOP, THE BIG BASEMENT.
Limbo
Lustful
Gluttonous
Avaricious & Prodigal
Wrathful & the Sullen
City of Dis Heretics Welcome
Violence
Fraudulence and Malice
Cocytus

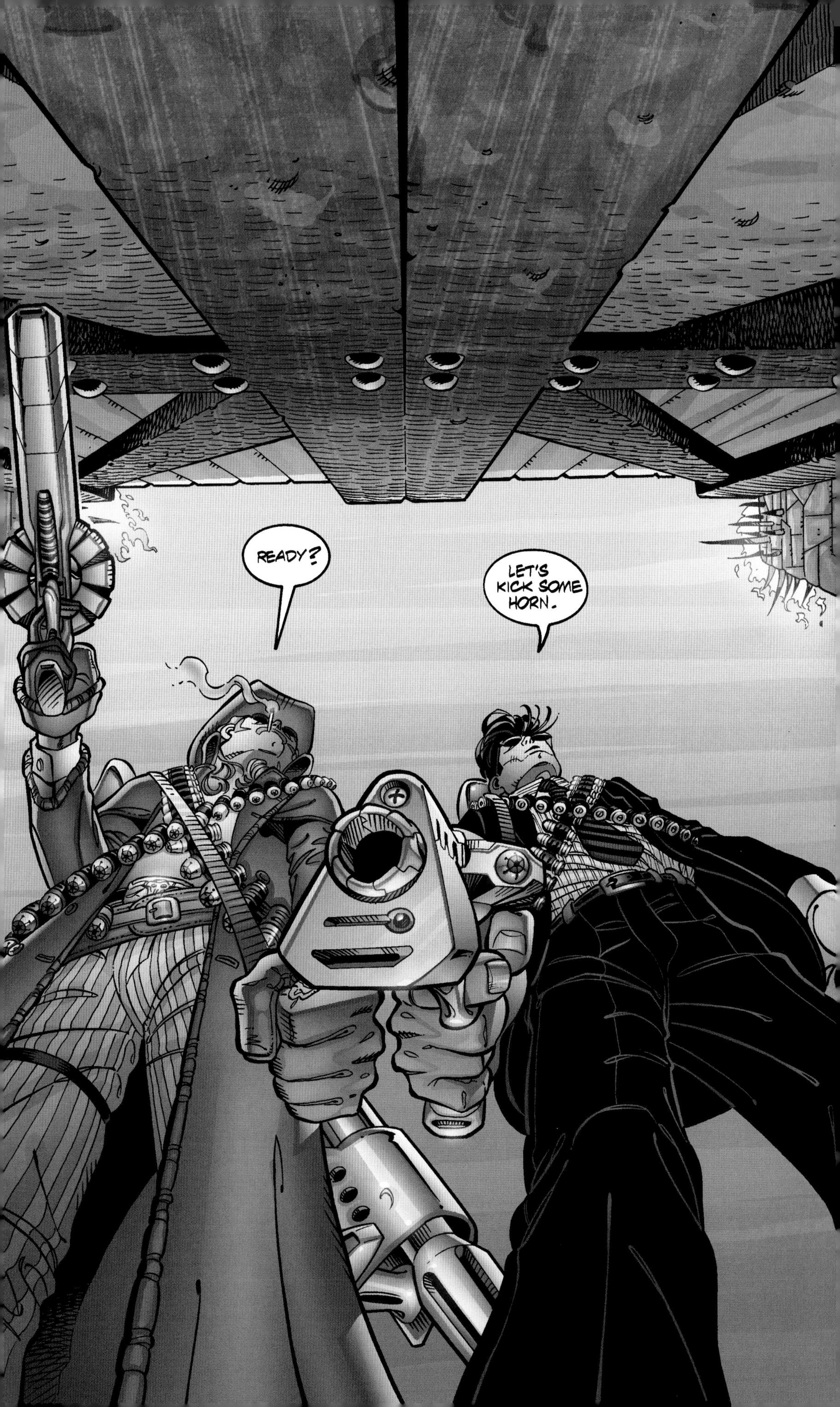
READY?
LET'S KICK SOME HORN.

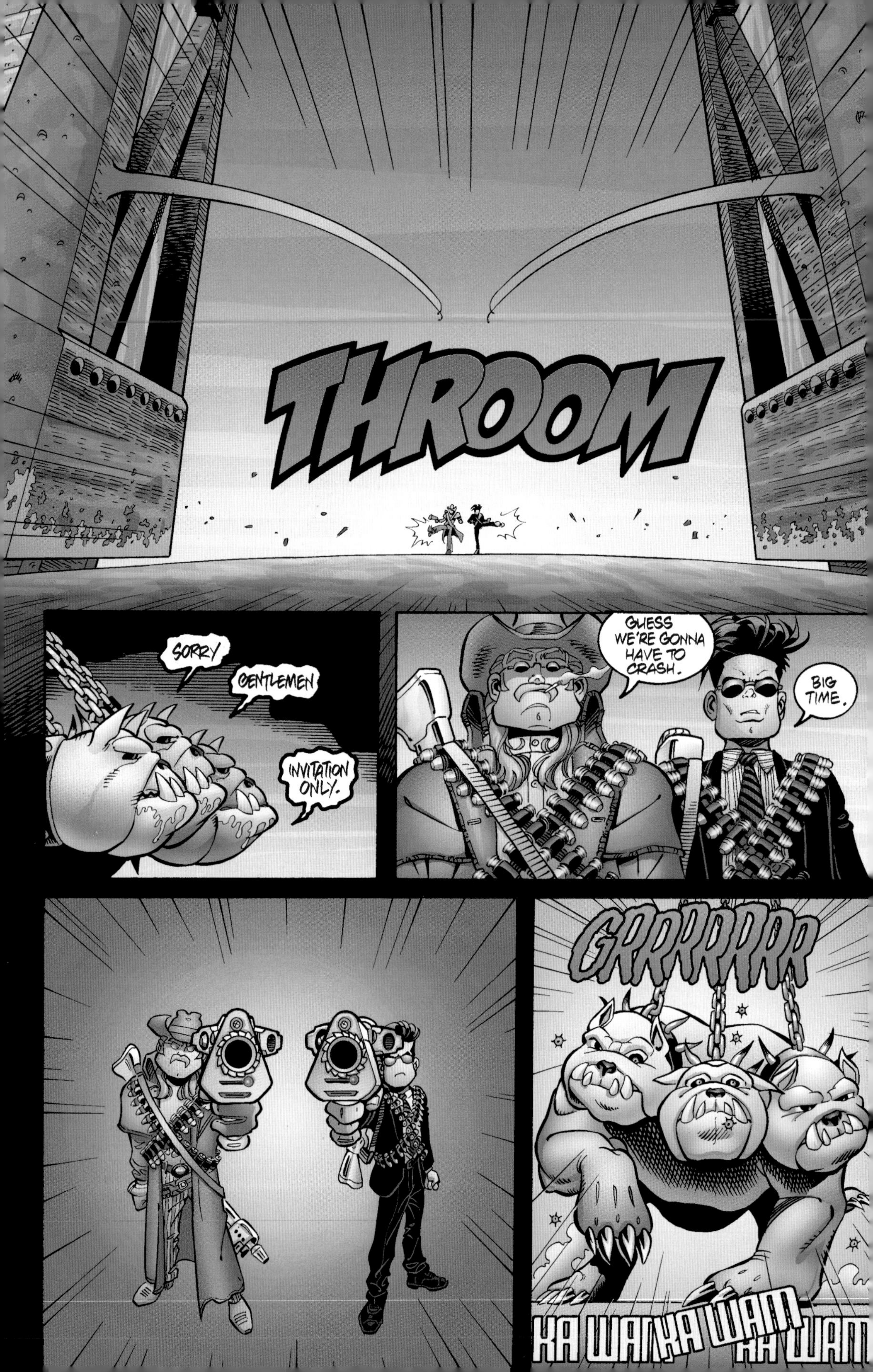
THROOM
SORRY
GENTLEMEN
INVITATION ONLY.
GUESS WE'RE GONNA HAVE TO CRASH.
BIG TIME.
GRRRRRRR
KA WAM KA WAM KA WAM

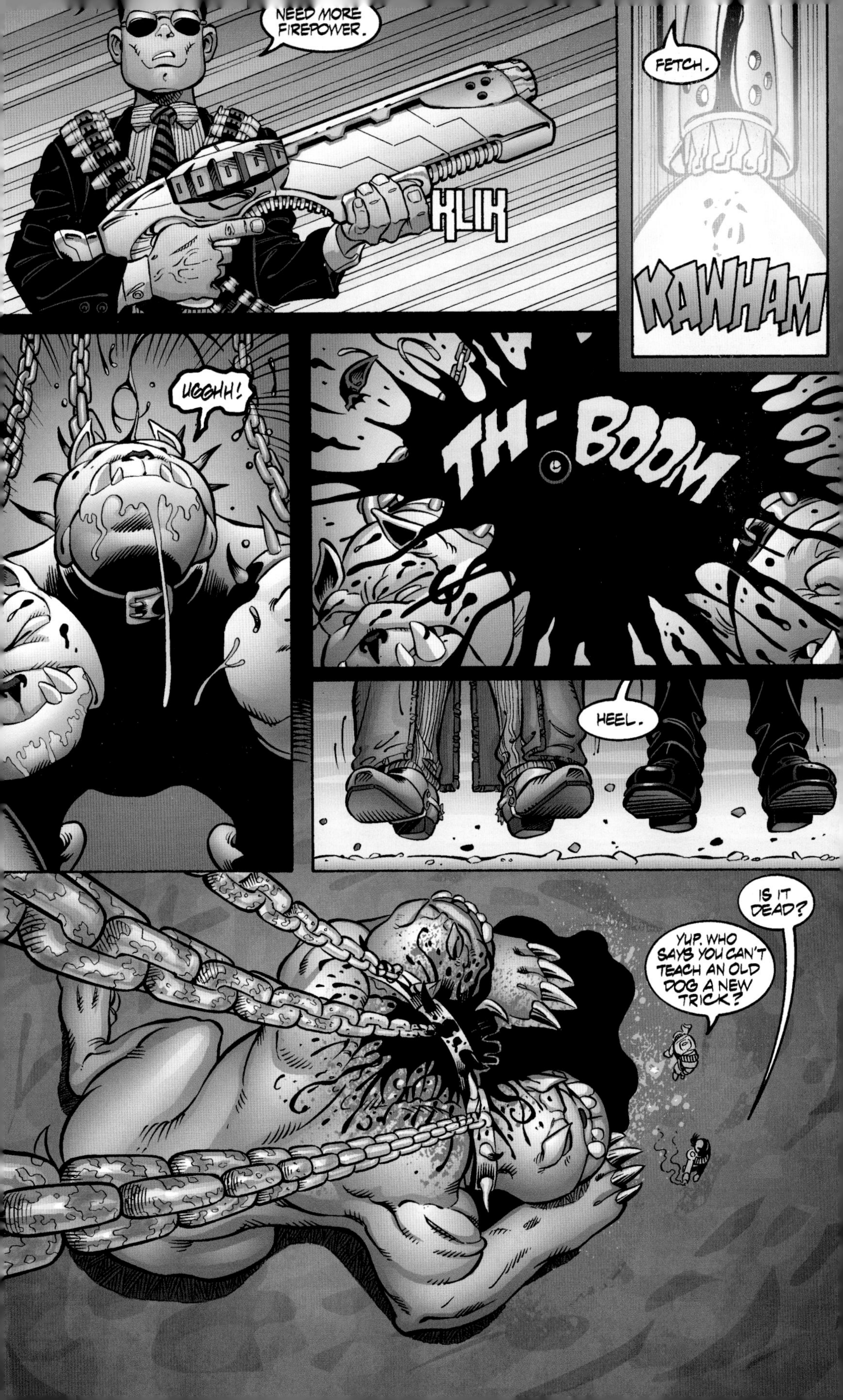
NEED MORE FIREPOWER.
KLIK
FETCH.
KAWHAM
UGGHH!
TH-BOOM
HEEL.
IS IT DEAD?
YUP. WHO SAYS YOU CAN'T TEACH AN OLD DOG A NEW TRICK?

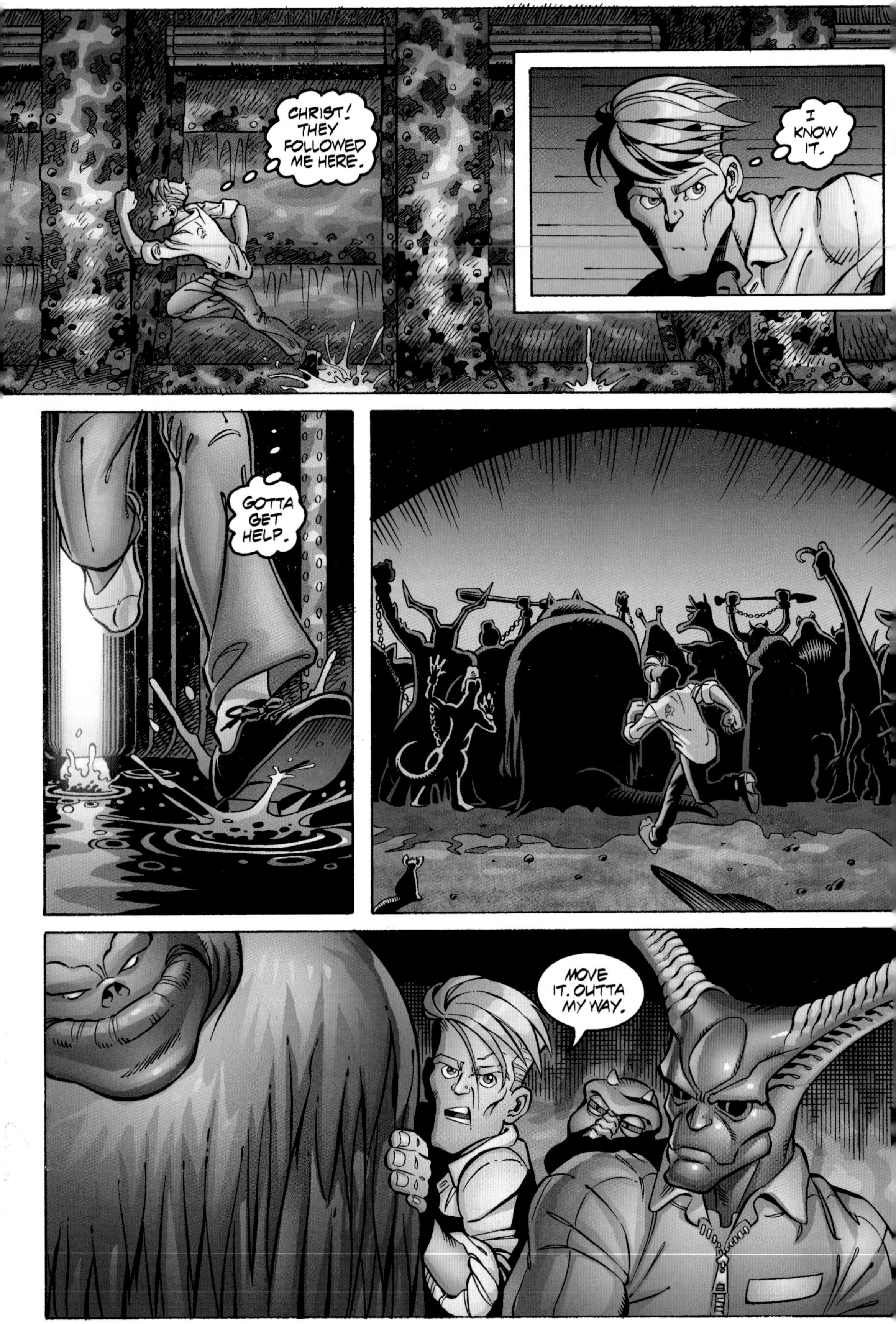
CHRIST! THEY FOLLOWED ME HERE.
I KNOW IT.
GOTTA GET HELP.
MOVE IT. OUTTA MY WAY.

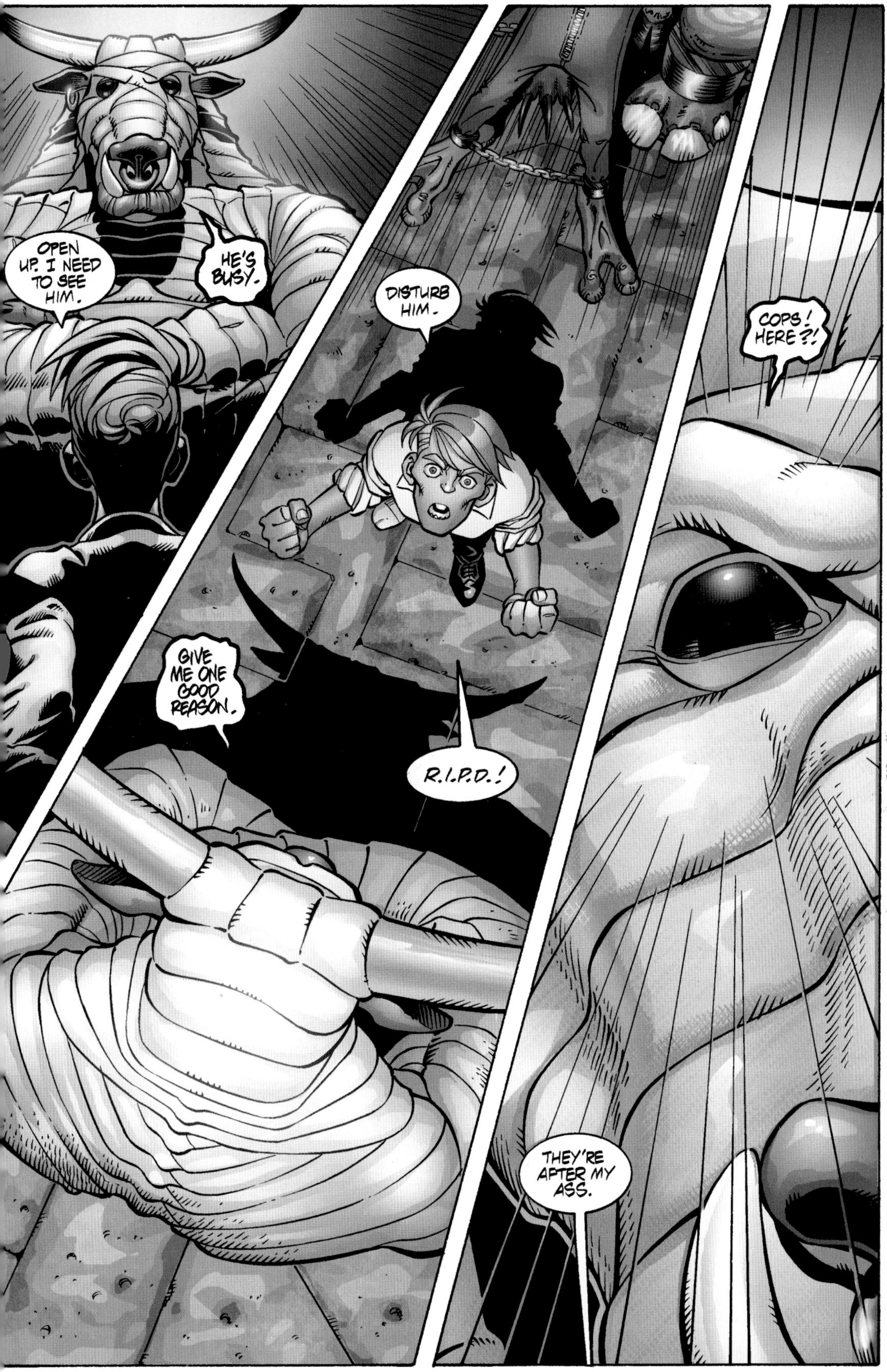
OPEN UP. I NEED TO SEE HIM.
HE'S BUSY.
DISTURB HIM.
GIVE ME ONE GOOD REASON.
R.I.P.D.!
COPS! HERE?!
THEY'RE AFTER MY ASS.

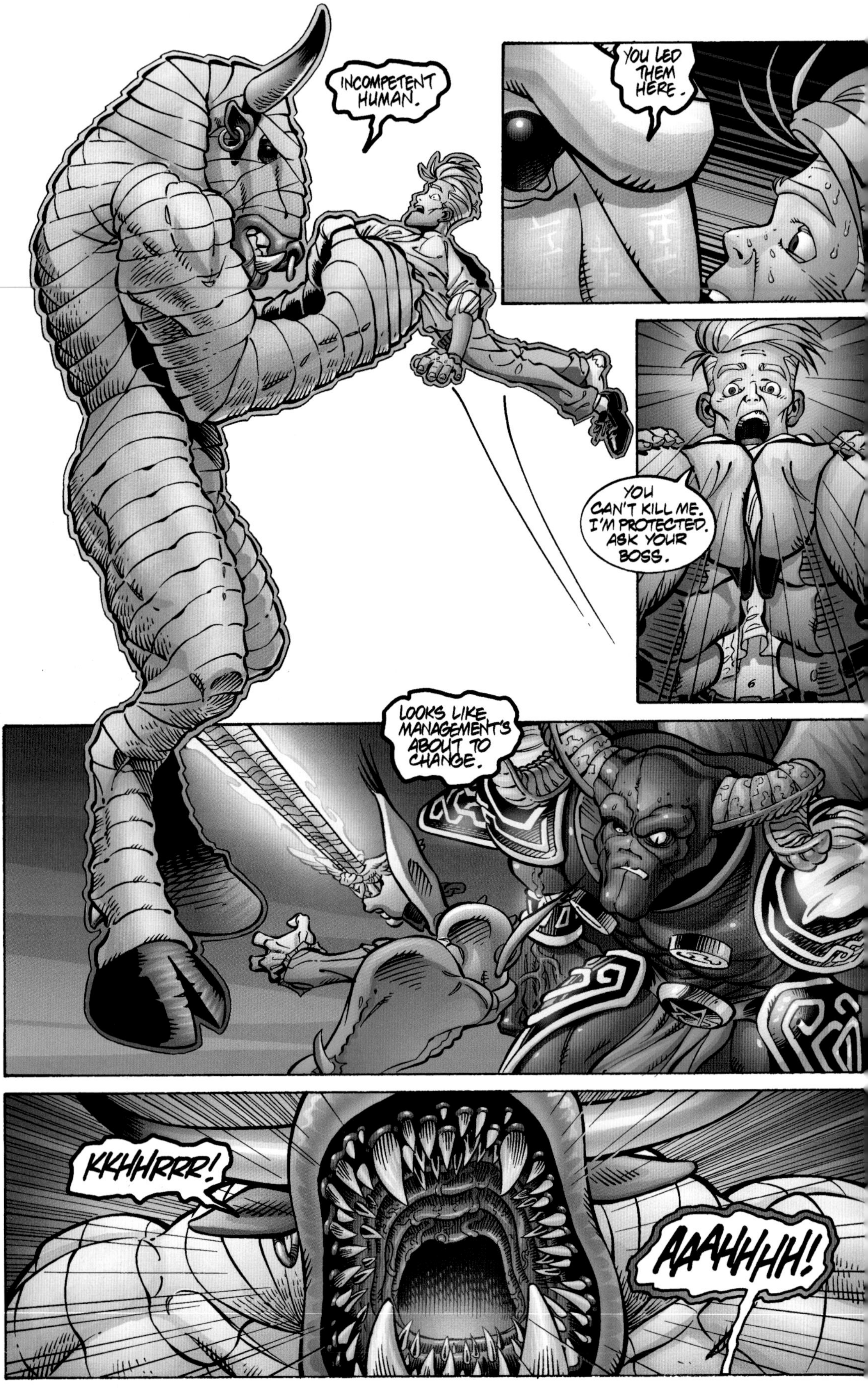
INCOMPETENT HUMAN.
YOU LED THEM HERE.
YOU CAN'T KILL ME. I'M PROTECTED. ASK YOUR BOSS.
LOOKS LIKE MANAGEMENT'S ABOUT TO CHANGE.
KKHHRRR!
AAAHHHH!

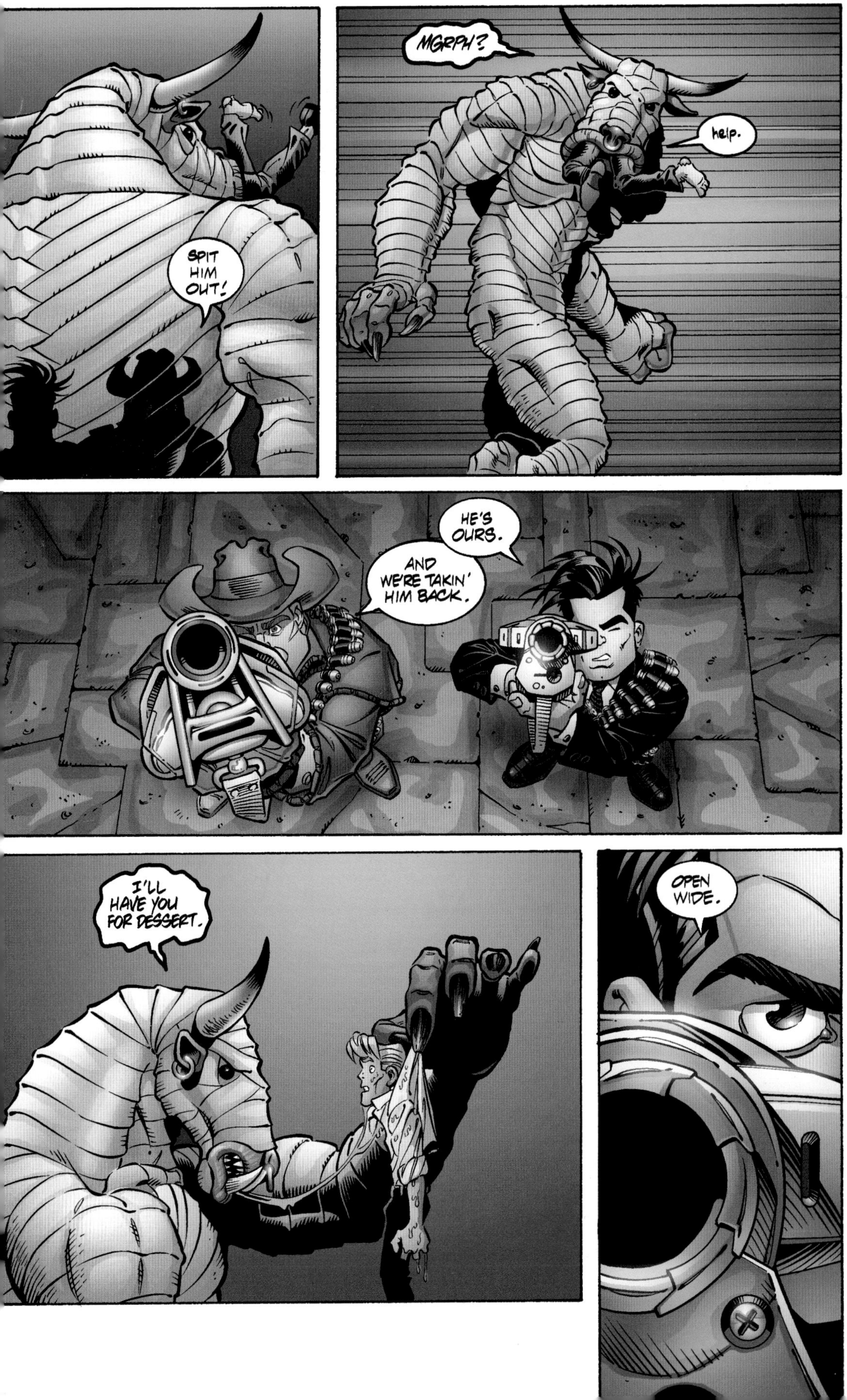
SPIT HIM OUT!
MGRPH?
help.
HE'S OURS.
AND WE'RE TAKIN' HIM BACK.
I'LL HAVE YOU FOR DESSERT.
OPEN WIDE.

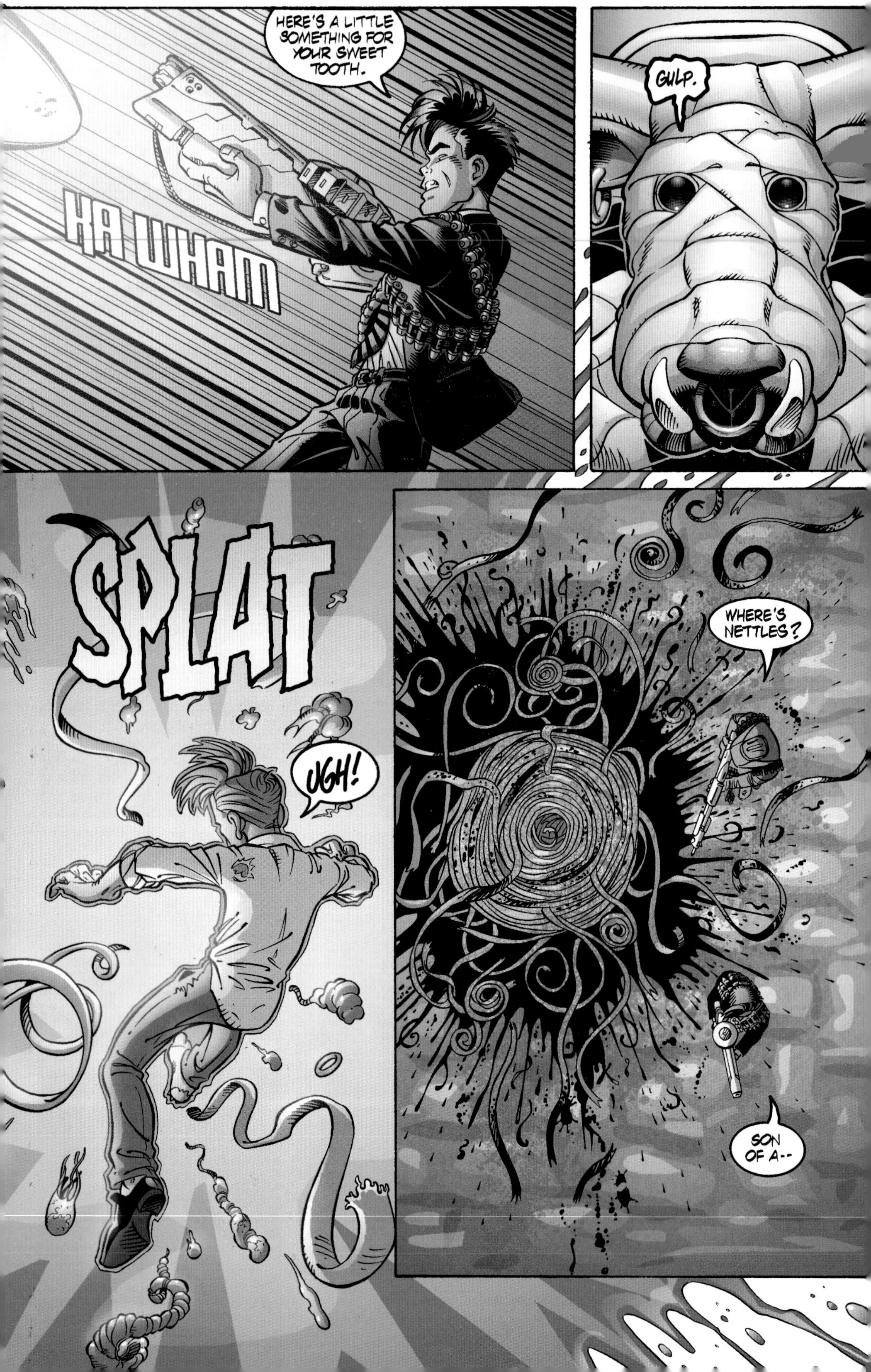
HERE'S A LITTLE SOMETHING FOR YOUR SWEET TOOTH.
KA WHAM
GULP.
SPLAT
UGH!
WHERE'S NETTLES?
SON OF A--

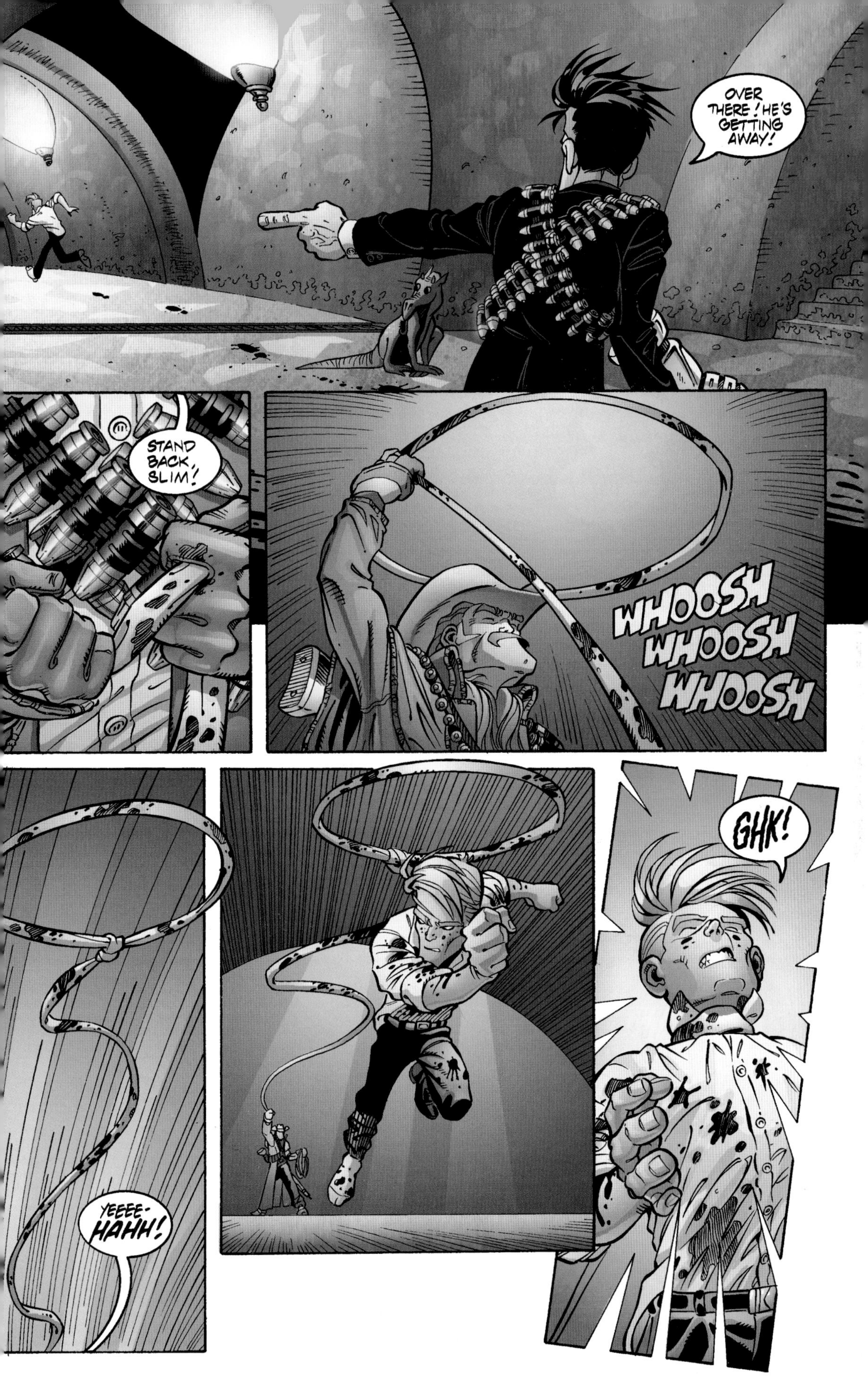
OVER THERE! HE'S GETTING AWAY!
STAND BACK, SLIM!
WHOOSH
WHOOSH
WHOOSH
YEEEE-HAHH!
GHK!

AH!

G'HEAD. KILL ME.

RETURN THE FAVOR.

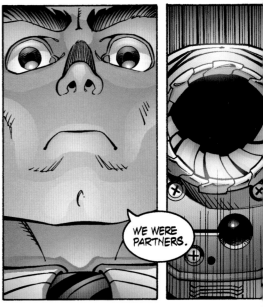

WE WERE PARTNERS.

LIFE'S A BITCH.

THEN YOU DIE.

NOT LIKE THIS. HE'LL PAY. DEARLY.

BUT NOT LIKE THIS.

YOU WON. WHY DON'T YOU JUST LEAVE ME HERE?

OH, YOU'LL BE BACK. GUARANTEED. BUT FIRST WE'RE GONNA BURY YOUR HIDE.

tchak

BURY?

WE'RE GONNA PIN A FEW MAJOR ATROCITIES ON YOU. ACTS OF GOD.

MAKE SURE WHEN YOU RETURN, YOUR STAY HERE ISN'T SO PLEASANT.

YO, POWELL, YOU BETTER COME TAKE A LOOK AT THIS.

IS THAT?

MICHAEL'S SWORD? YEP.

LOOKS LIKE SOMEONE'S MAKIN' A POWER PLAY.

THUD

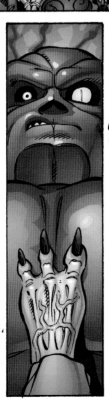

VIVA LA REVOLUCIÓN!

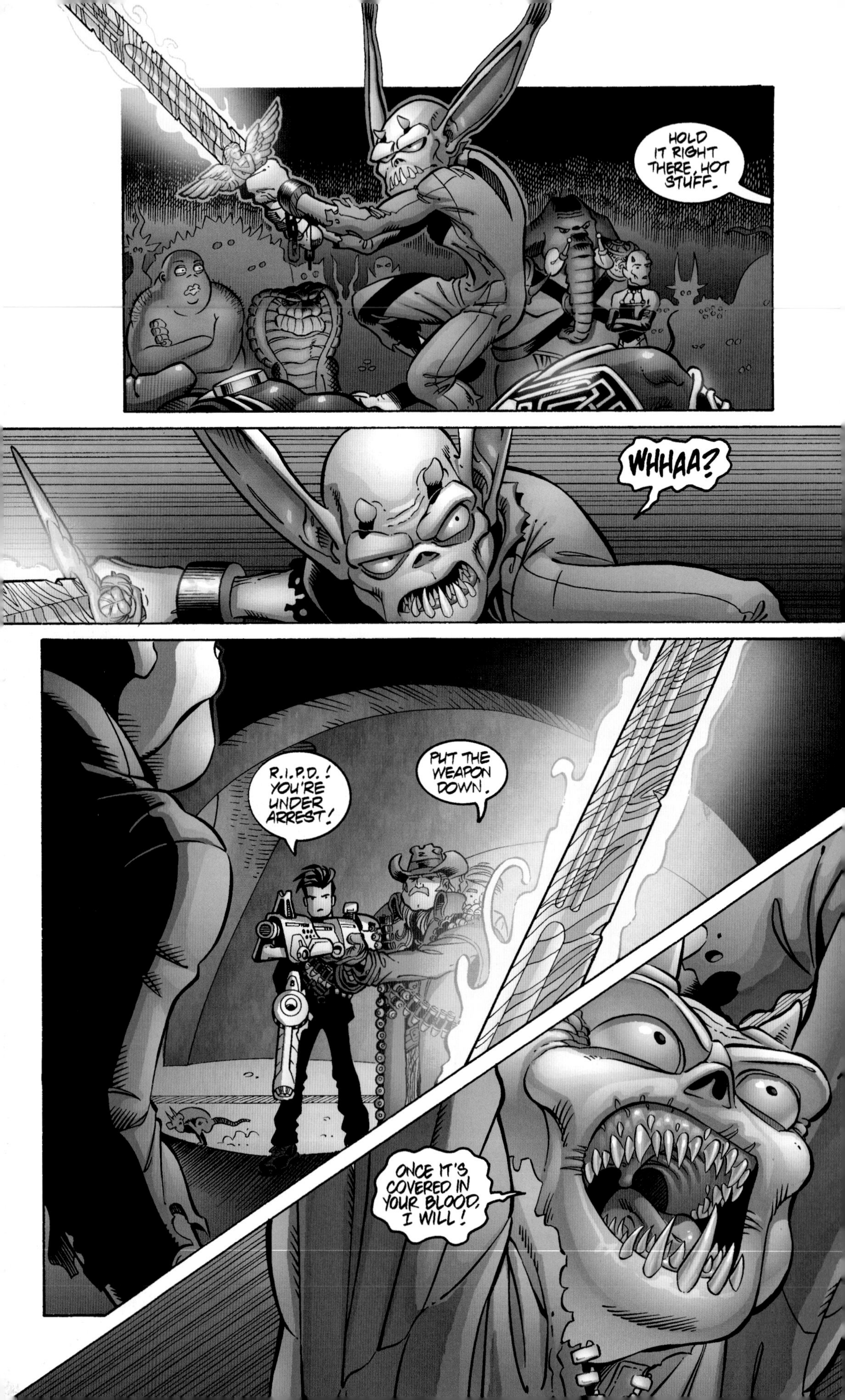
HOLD IT RIGHT THERE, HOT STUFF.
WHHAA?
R.I.P.D.! YOU'RE UNDER ARREST!
PUT THE WEAPON DOWN.
ONCE IT'S COVERED IN YOUR BLOOD, I WILL!

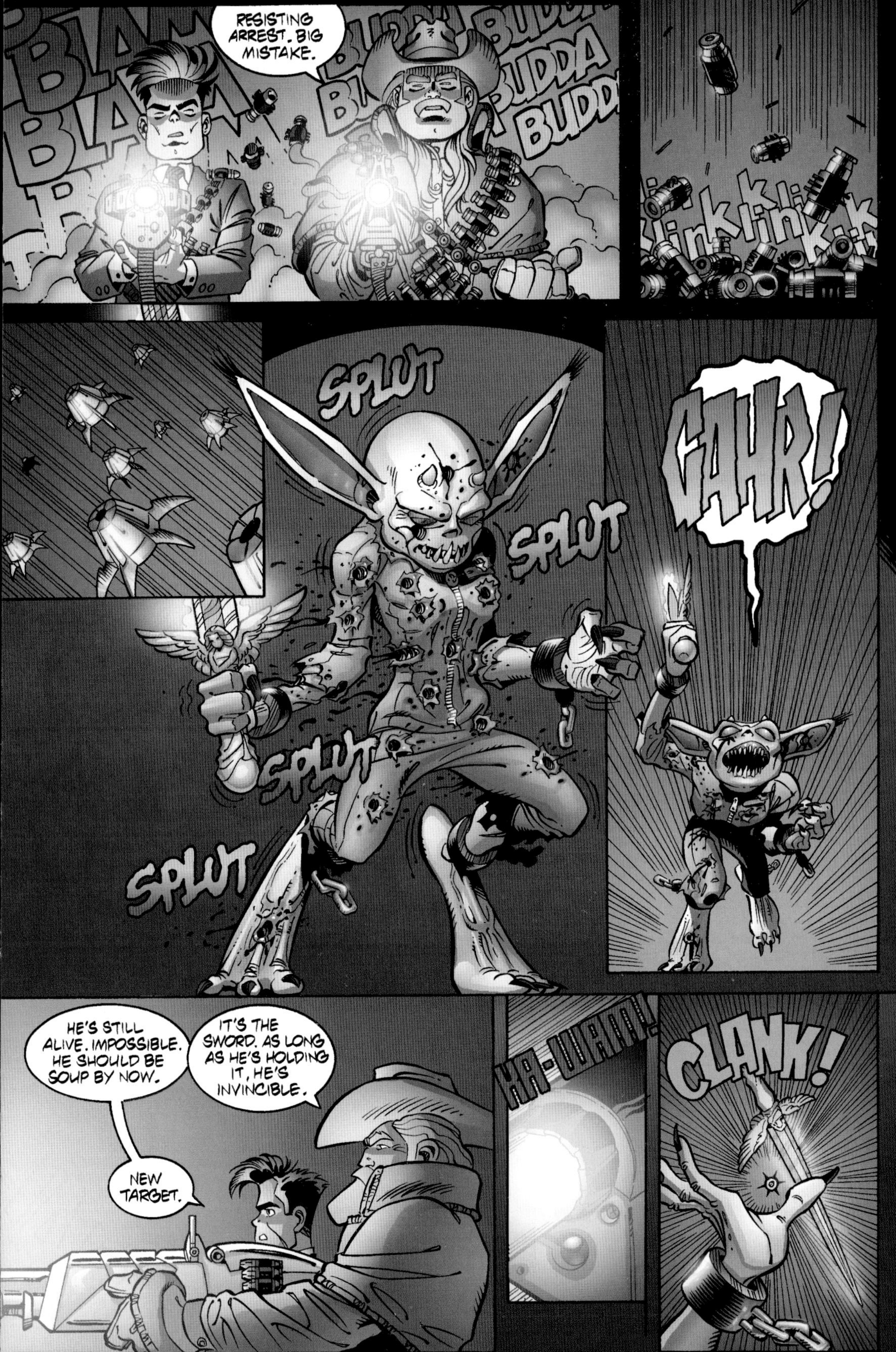
BLAM BLAM
RESISTING ARREST. BIG MISTAKE.
BUDDA BUDDA BUDDA BUDDA
klink klink klink
SPLUT
SPLUT
CAHR!
SPLUT
SPLUT
HE'S STILL ALIVE. IMPOSSIBLE. HE SHOULD BE SOUP BY NOW.
IT'S THE SWORD. AS LONG AS HE'S HOLDING IT, HE'S INVINCIBLE.
NEW TARGET.
KA-WAM!
CLANK!

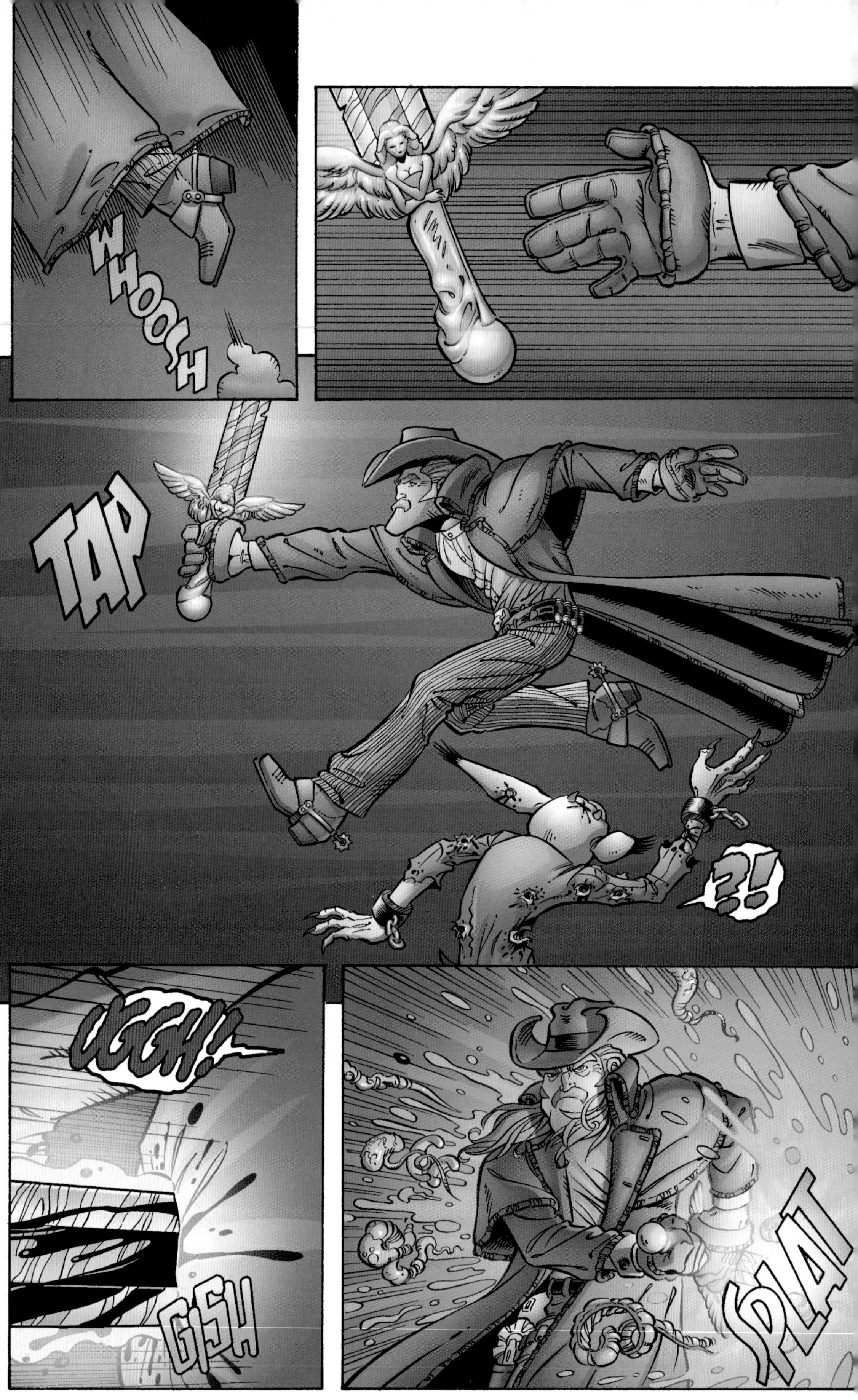
WHOOSH
TAP
?!
UGGH!
GISH
SPLAT

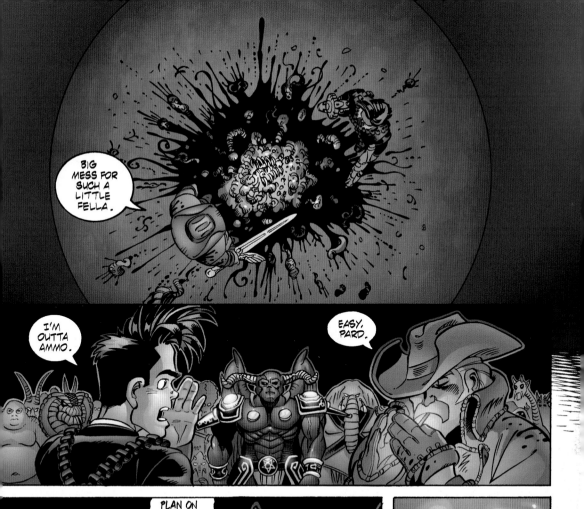

BIG MESS FOR SUCH A LITTLE FELLA.

I'M OUTTA AMMO.

EASY, PARD.

PLAN ON USING THAT THING?

NOT RIGHT AWAY.

YOU SAVED MY LIFE. WHAT'S YOUR BOSS GONNA SAY?

HE'S PATIENT. THERE WILL BE ANOTHER DAY.

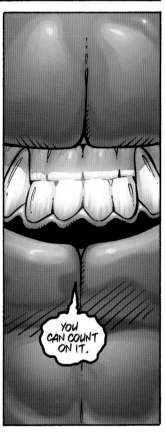

YOU CAN COUNT ON IT.

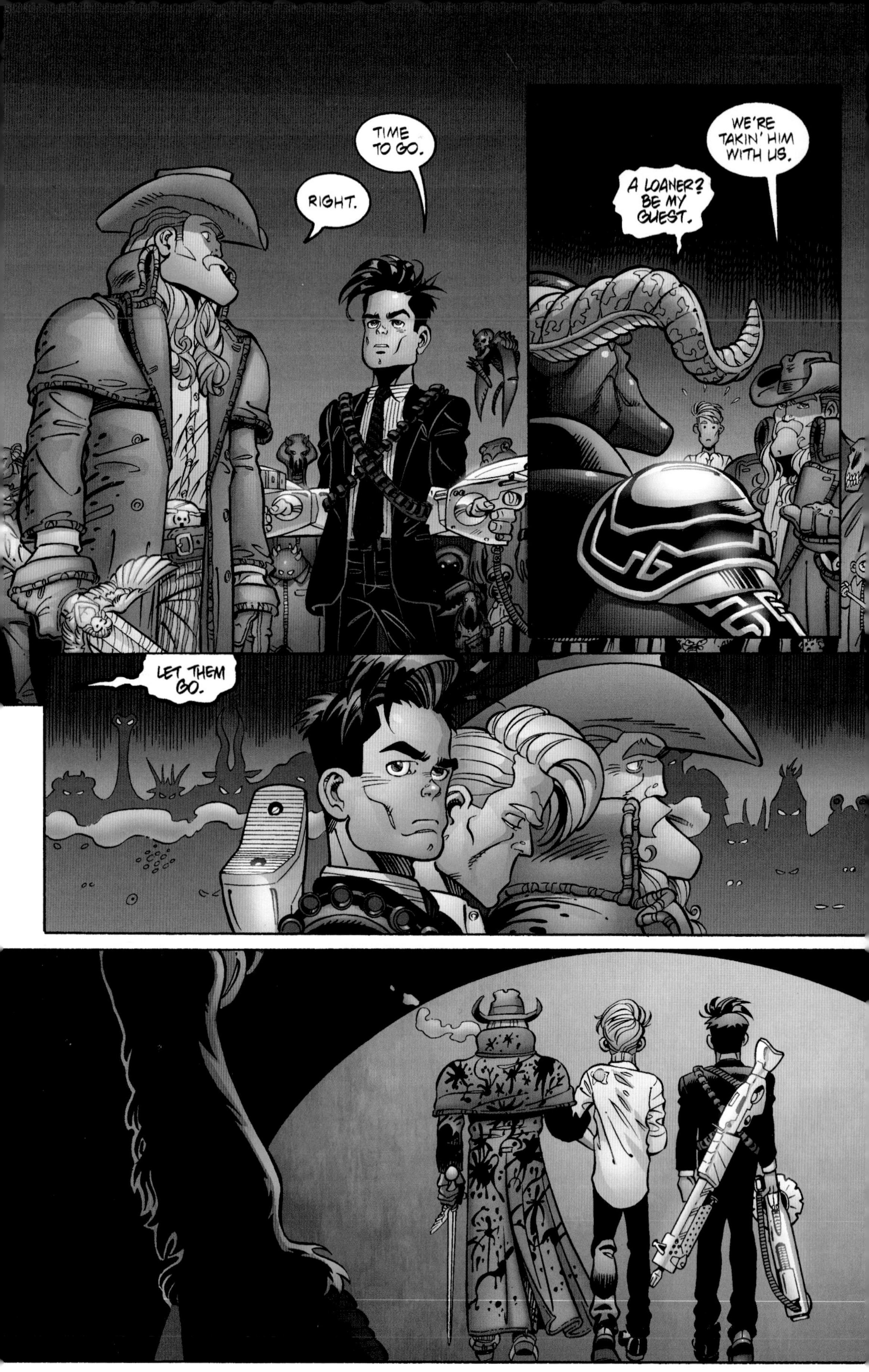

TIME TO GO.
RIGHT.
WE'RE TAKIN' HIM WITH US.
A LOANER? BE MY GUEST.
LET THEM GO.

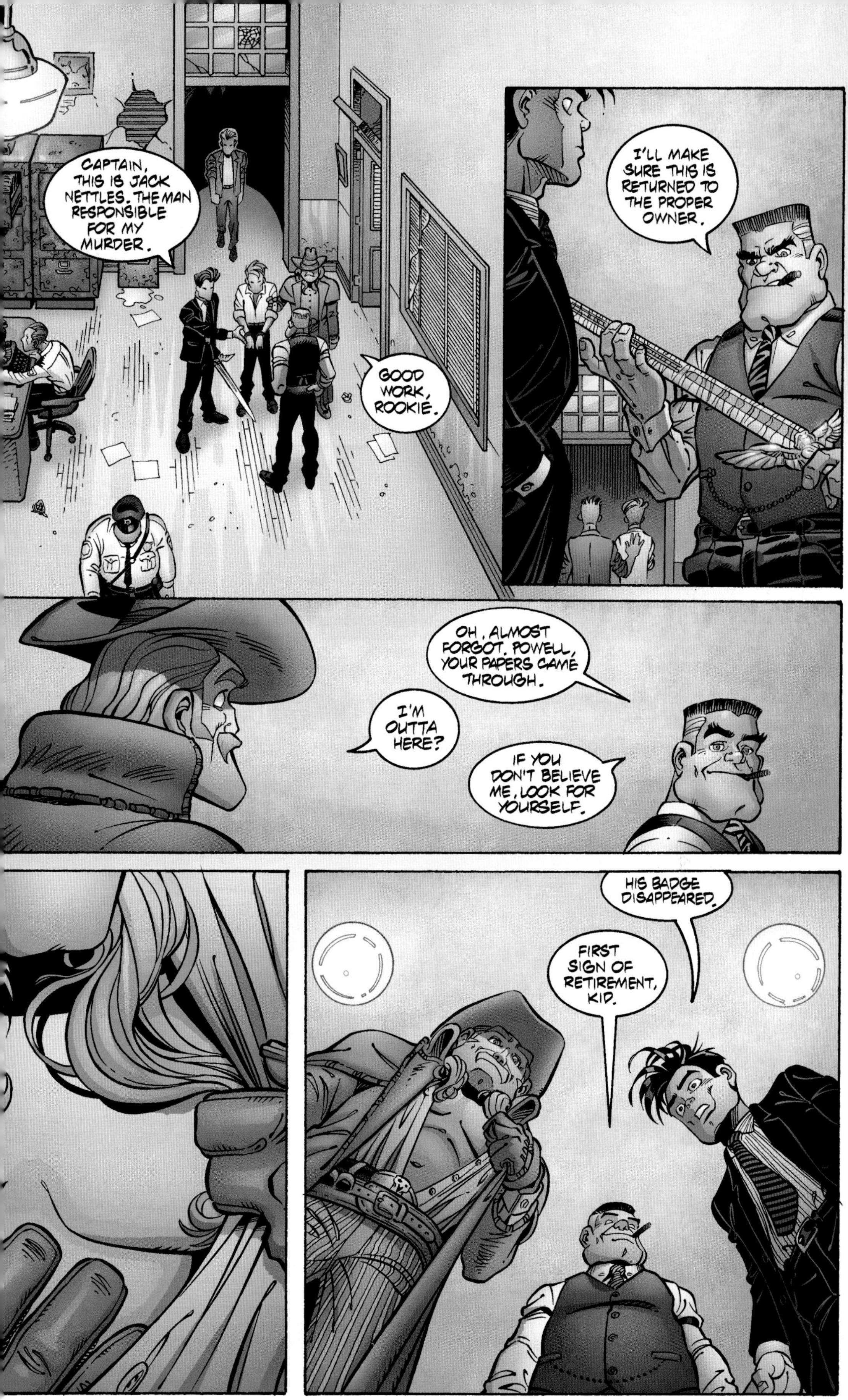
CAPTAIN, THIS IS JACK NETTLES. THE MAN RESPONSIBLE FOR MY MURDER.
GOOD WORK, ROOKIE.
I'LL MAKE SURE THIS IS RETURNED TO THE PROPER OWNER.
OH, ALMOST FORGOT. POWELL, YOUR PAPERS CAME THROUGH.
I'M OUTTA HERE?
IF YOU DON'T BELIEVE ME, LOOK FOR YOURSELF.
HIS BADGE DISAPPEARED.
FIRST SIGN OF RETIREMENT, KID.

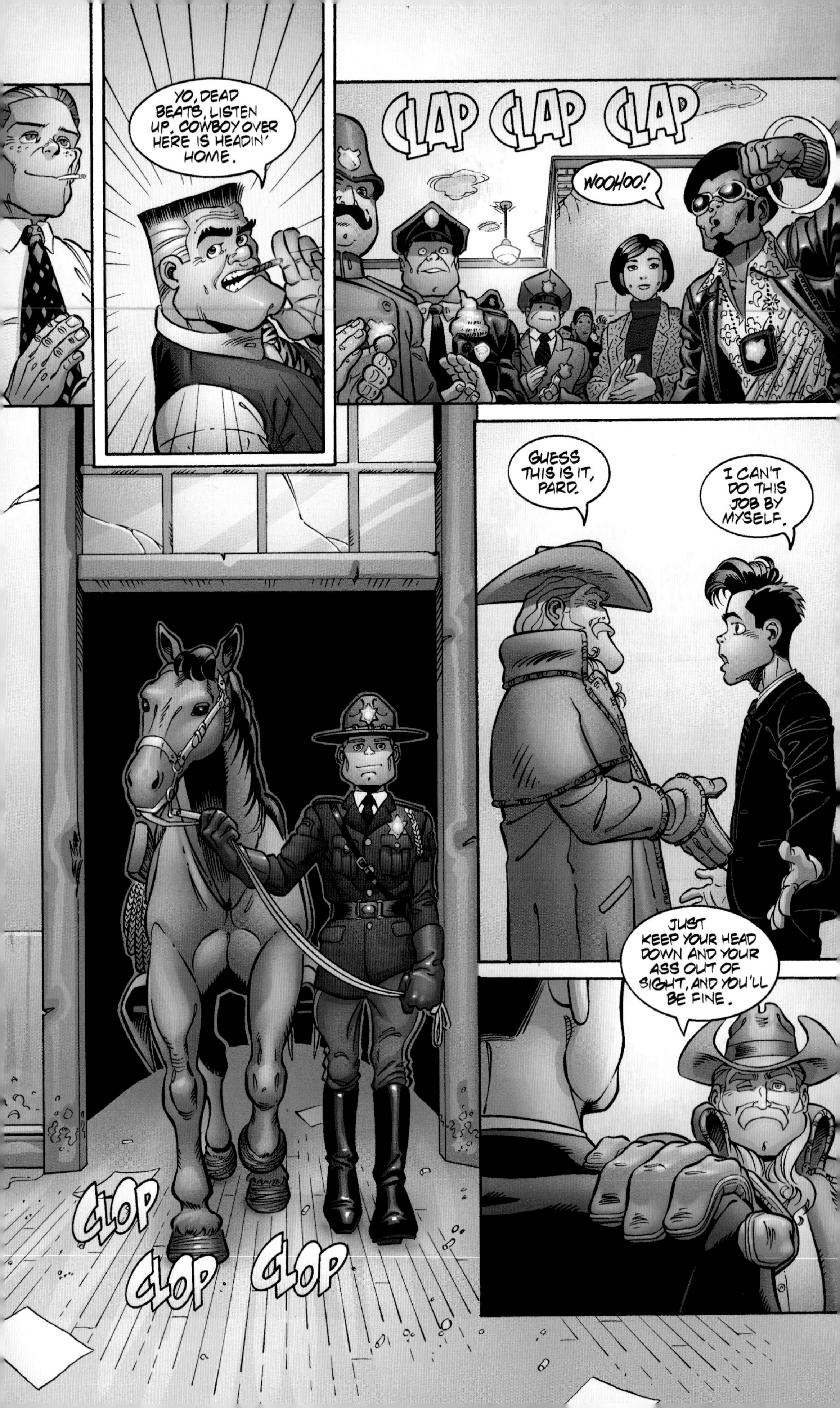
YO, DEAD BEATS, LISTEN UP. COWBOY OVER HERE IS HEADIN' HOME.
CLAP CLAP CLAP
WOOHOO!
CLOP
CLOP CLOP
GUESS THIS IS IT, PARD.
I CAN'T DO THIS JOB BY MYSELF.
JUST KEEP YOUR HEAD DOWN AND YOUR ASS OUT OF SIGHT, AND YOU'LL BE FINE.

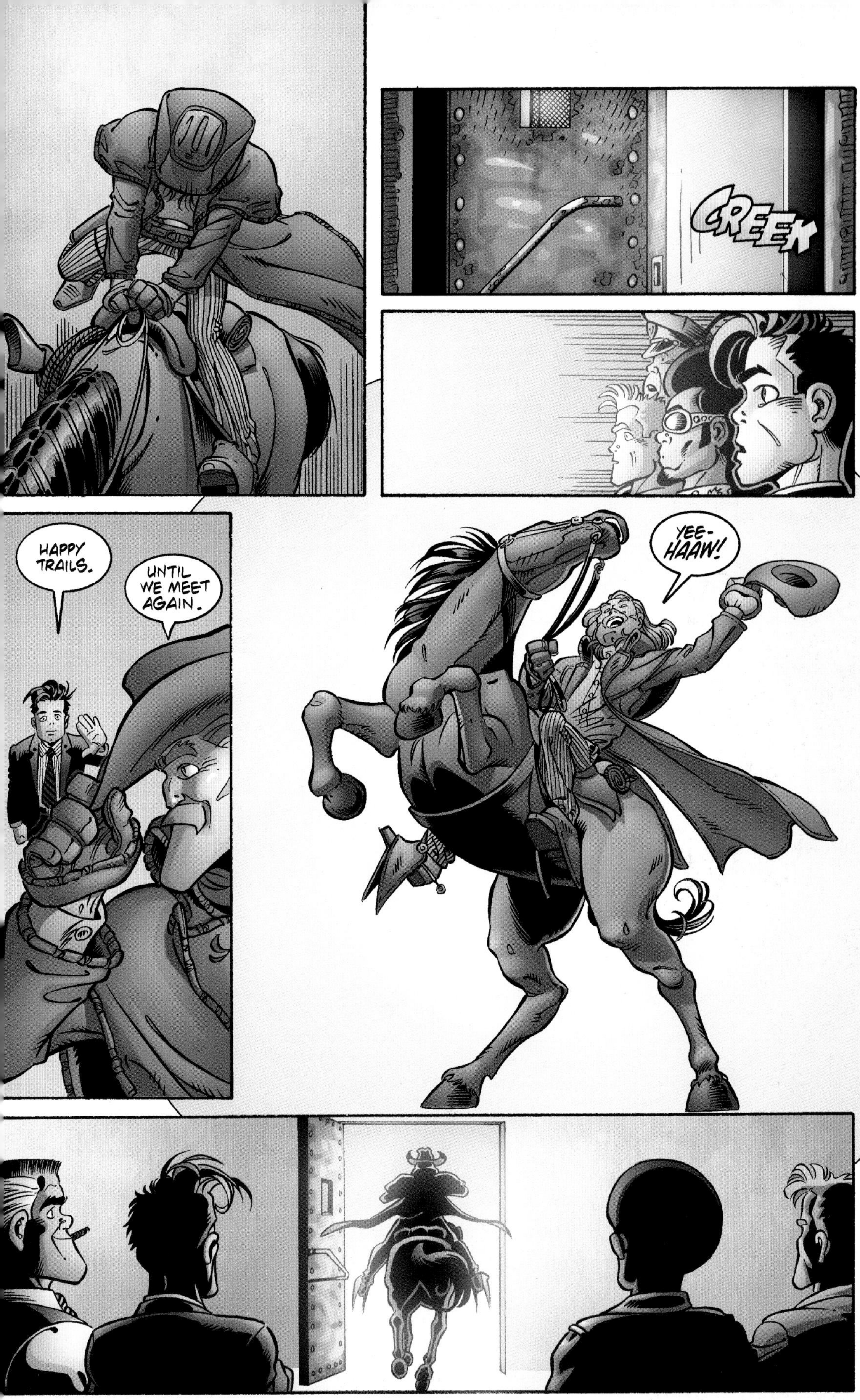
CREEK
HAPPY TRAILS.
UNTIL WE MEET AGAIN.
YEE-HAAW!

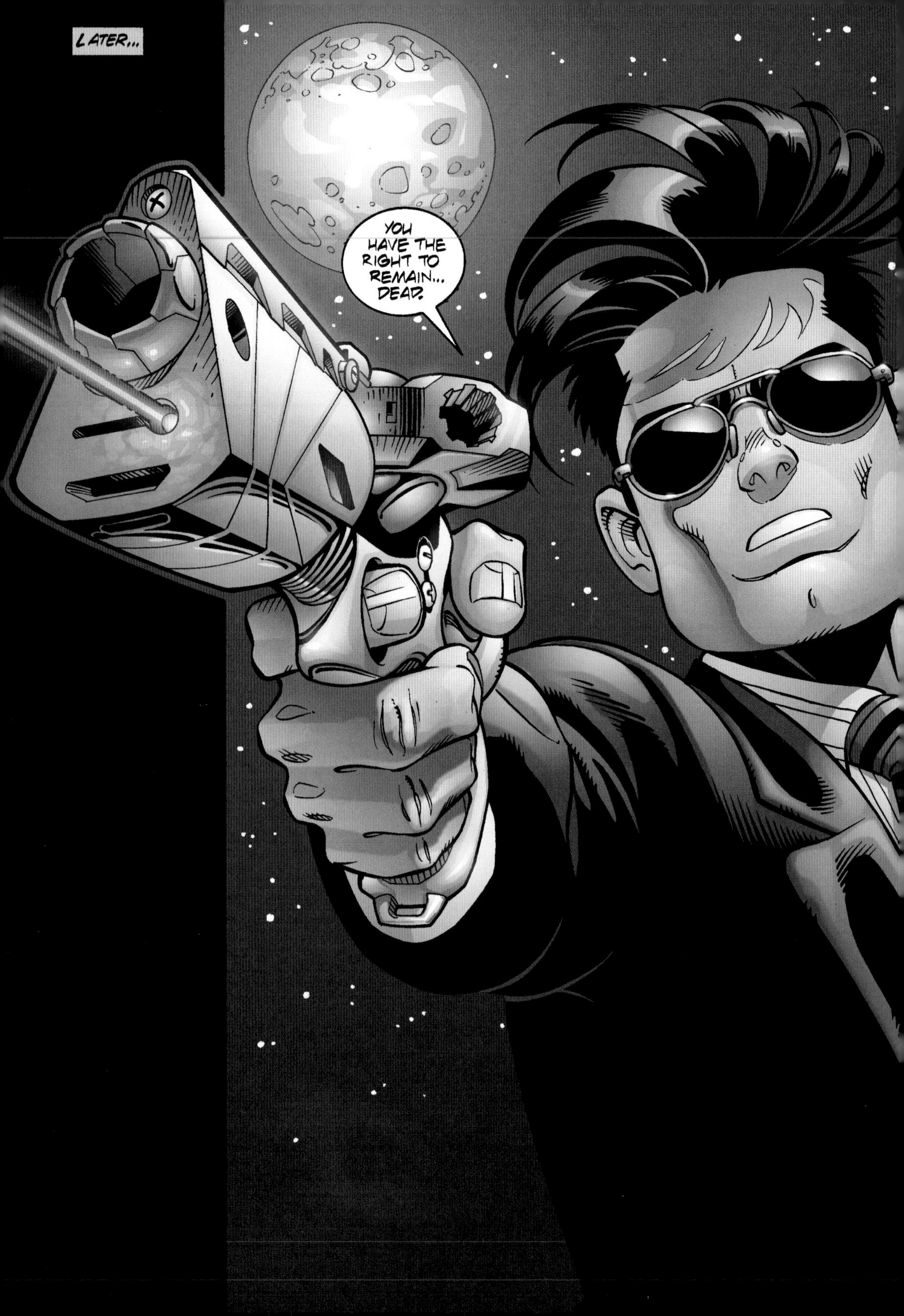
LATER...
YOU HAVE THE RIGHT TO REMAIN... DEAD.

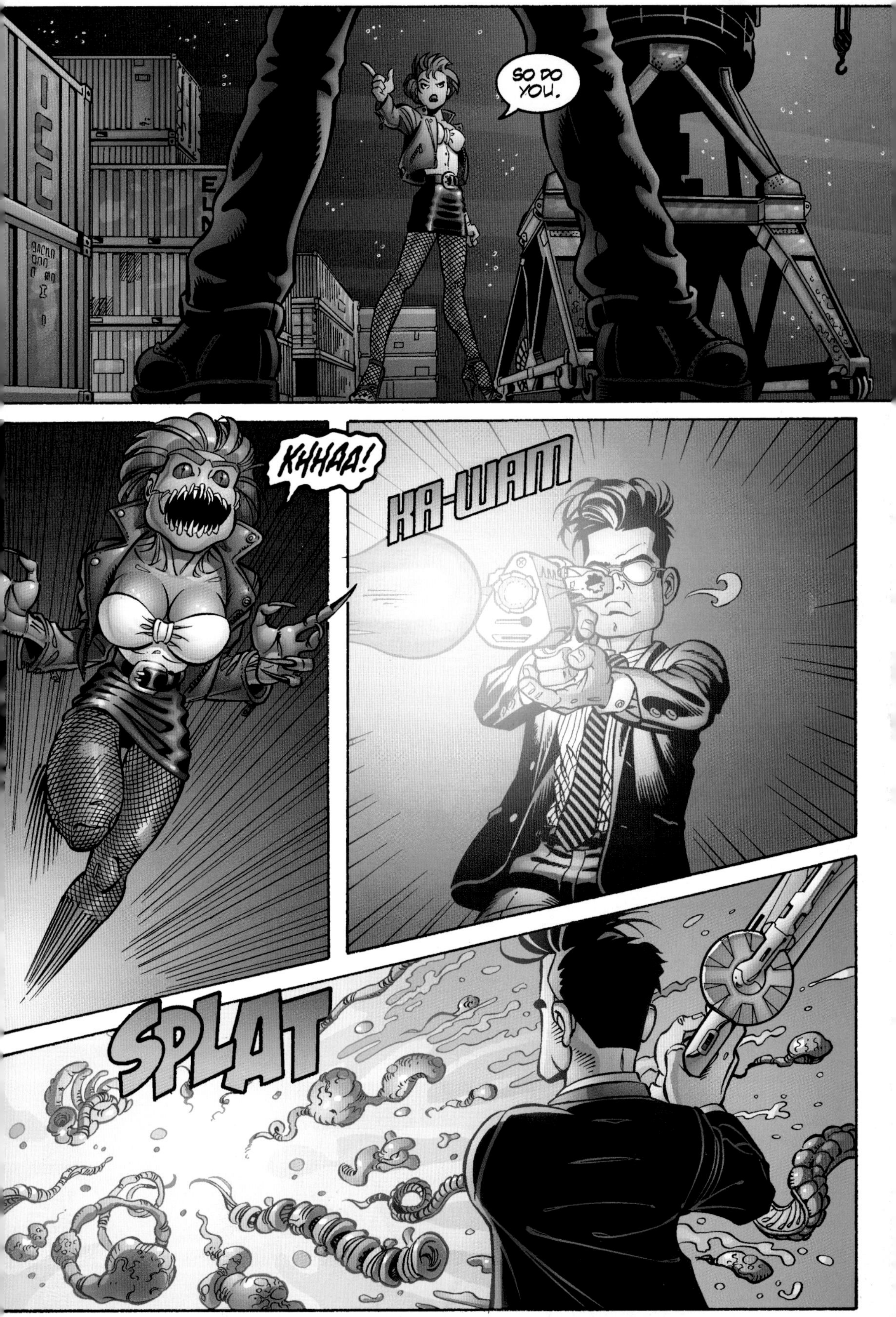
SO DO YOU.
KHHAA!
KA-WAM
SPLAT

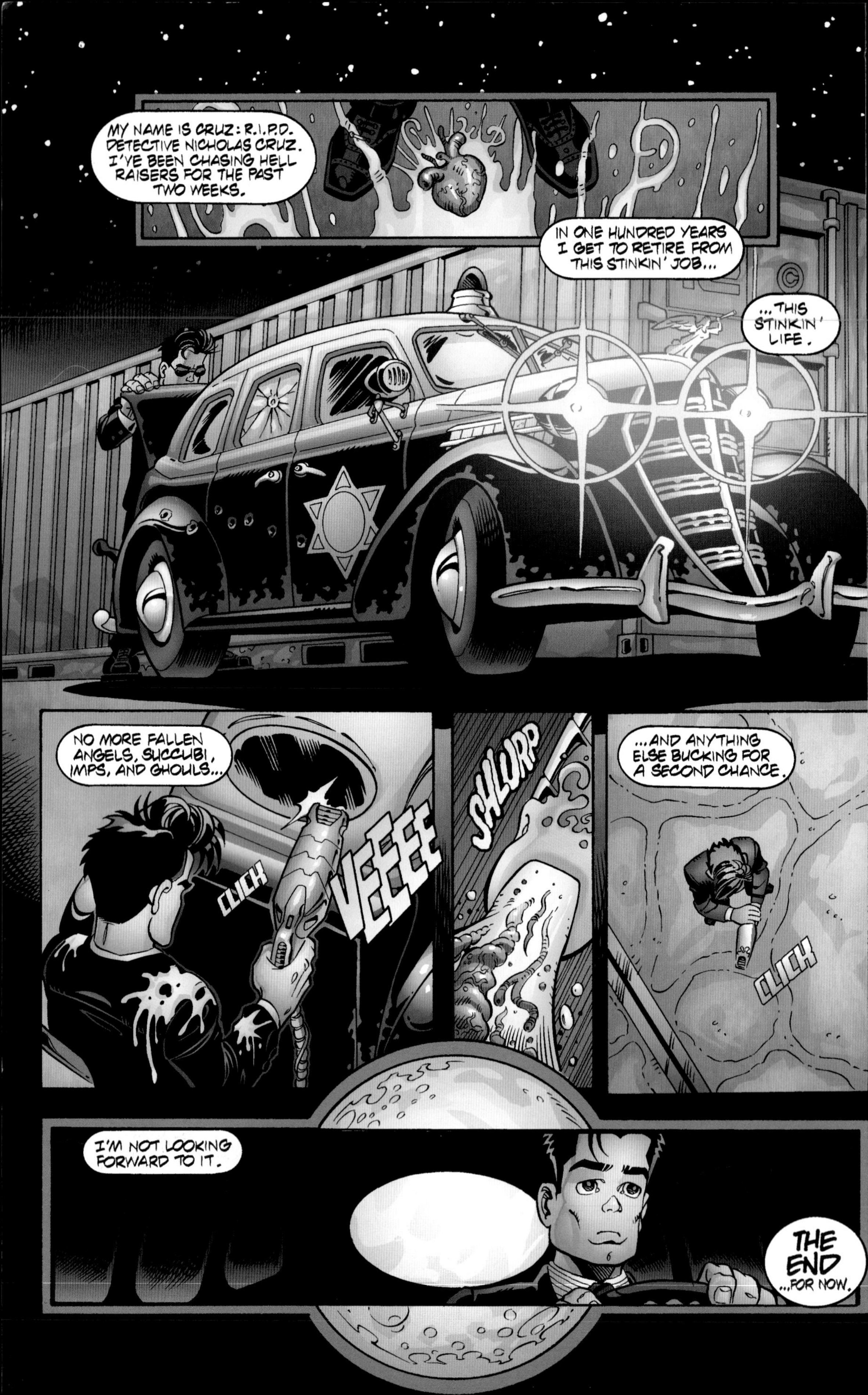
MY NAME IS CRUZ: R.I.P.D. DETECTIVE NICHOLAS CRUZ. I'VE BEEN CHASING HELL RAISERS FOR THE PAST TWO WEEKS.
IN ONE HUNDRED YEARS I GET TO RETIRE FROM THIS STINKIN' JOB...
...THIS STINKIN' LIFE.
NO MORE FALLEN ANGELS, SUCCUBI, IMPS, AND GHOULS...
CLICK
VEEEEE
SHLURP
...AND ANYTHING ELSE BUCKING FOR A SECOND CHANCE.
CLICK
I'M NOT LOOKING FORWARD TO IT.
THE END ...FOR NOW.

R.I.P.D. COVER GALLERY

Featuring cover art by LUCAS MARANGON and RANDY EMBERLIN, with colors by DAVE McCAIG.

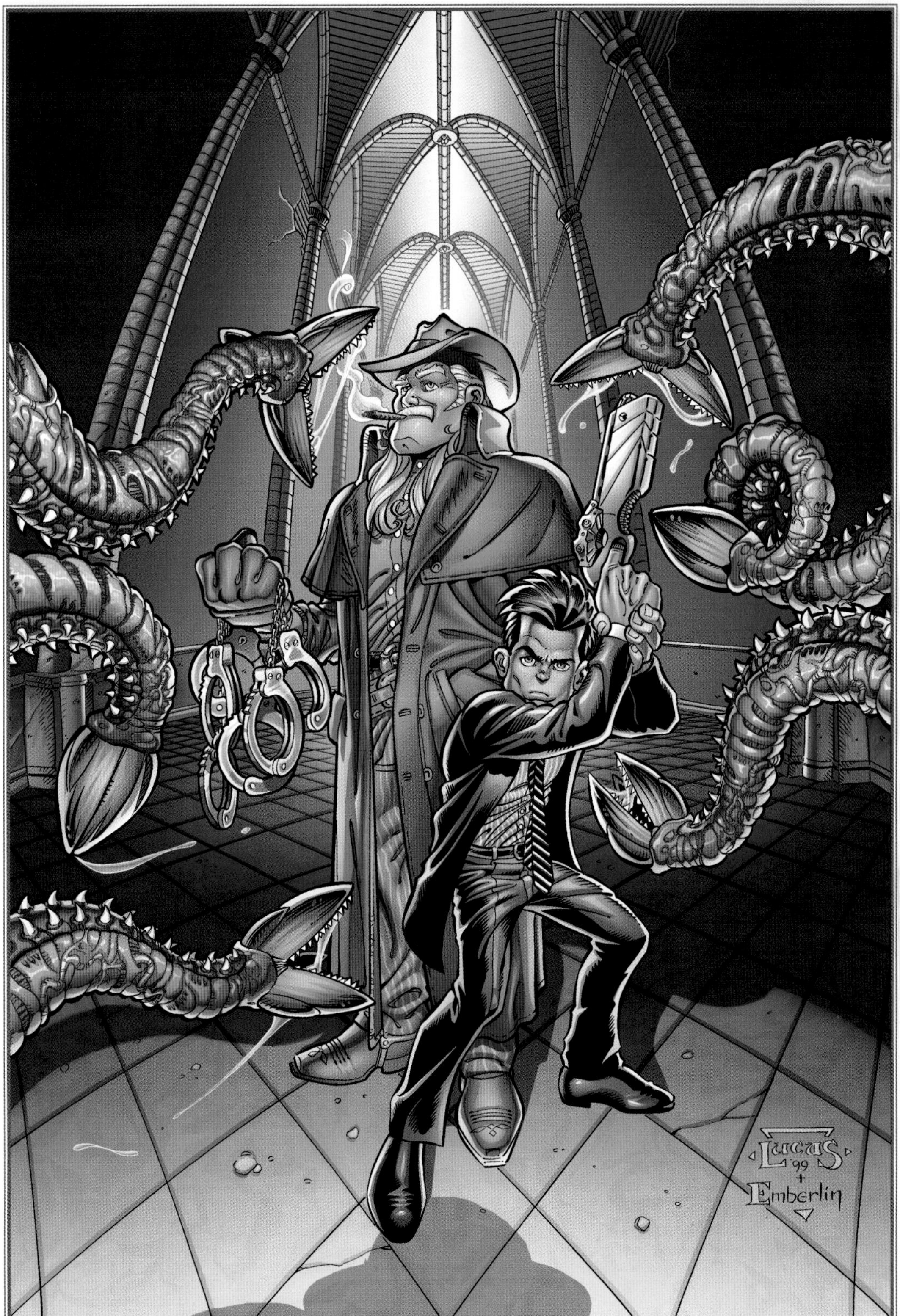

Lucas '99 + Emberlin

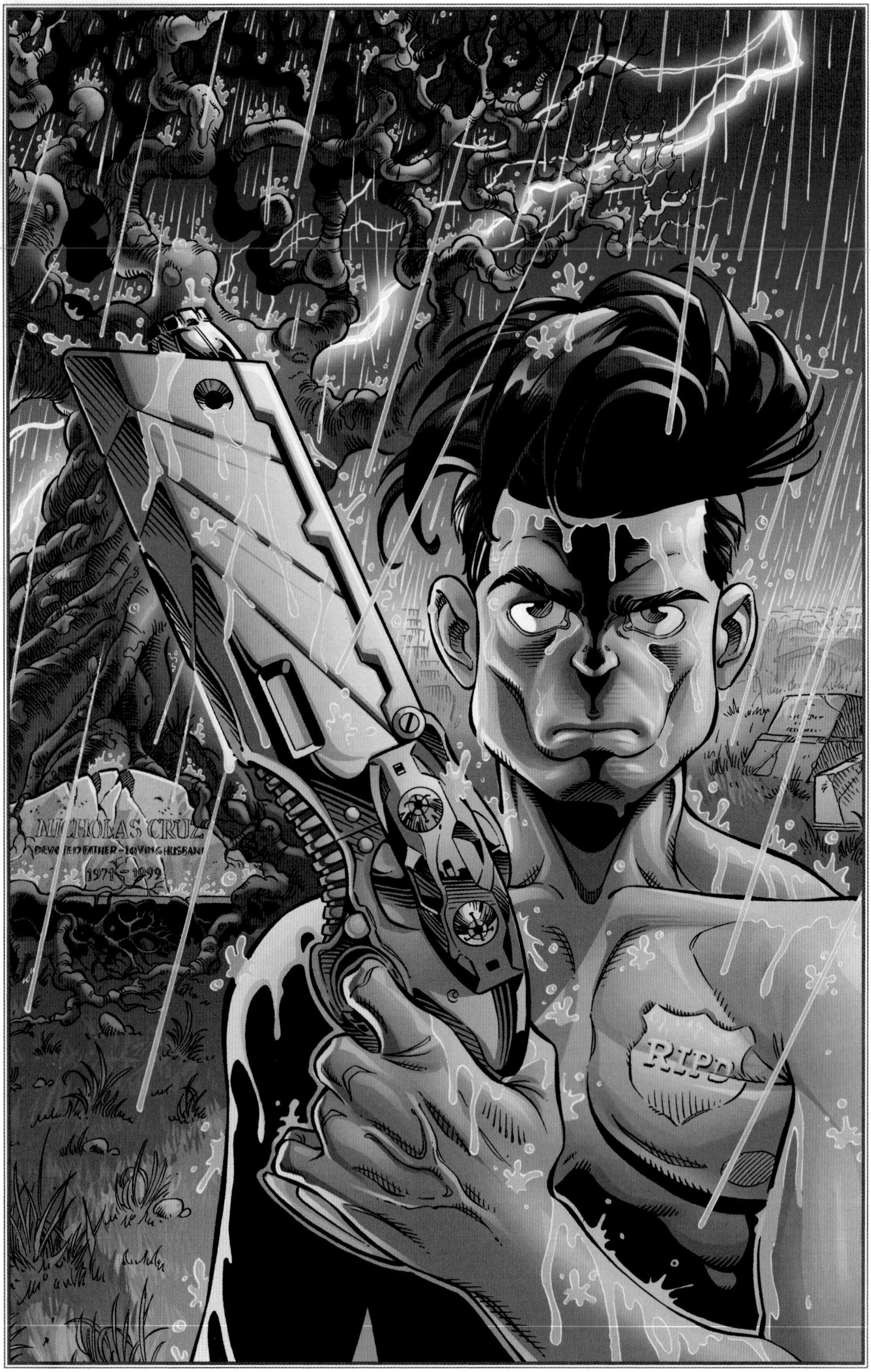
NICHOLAS CRUZ
DEVOTED FATHER - LOVING HUSBAND
1971 - 1999
RIPD

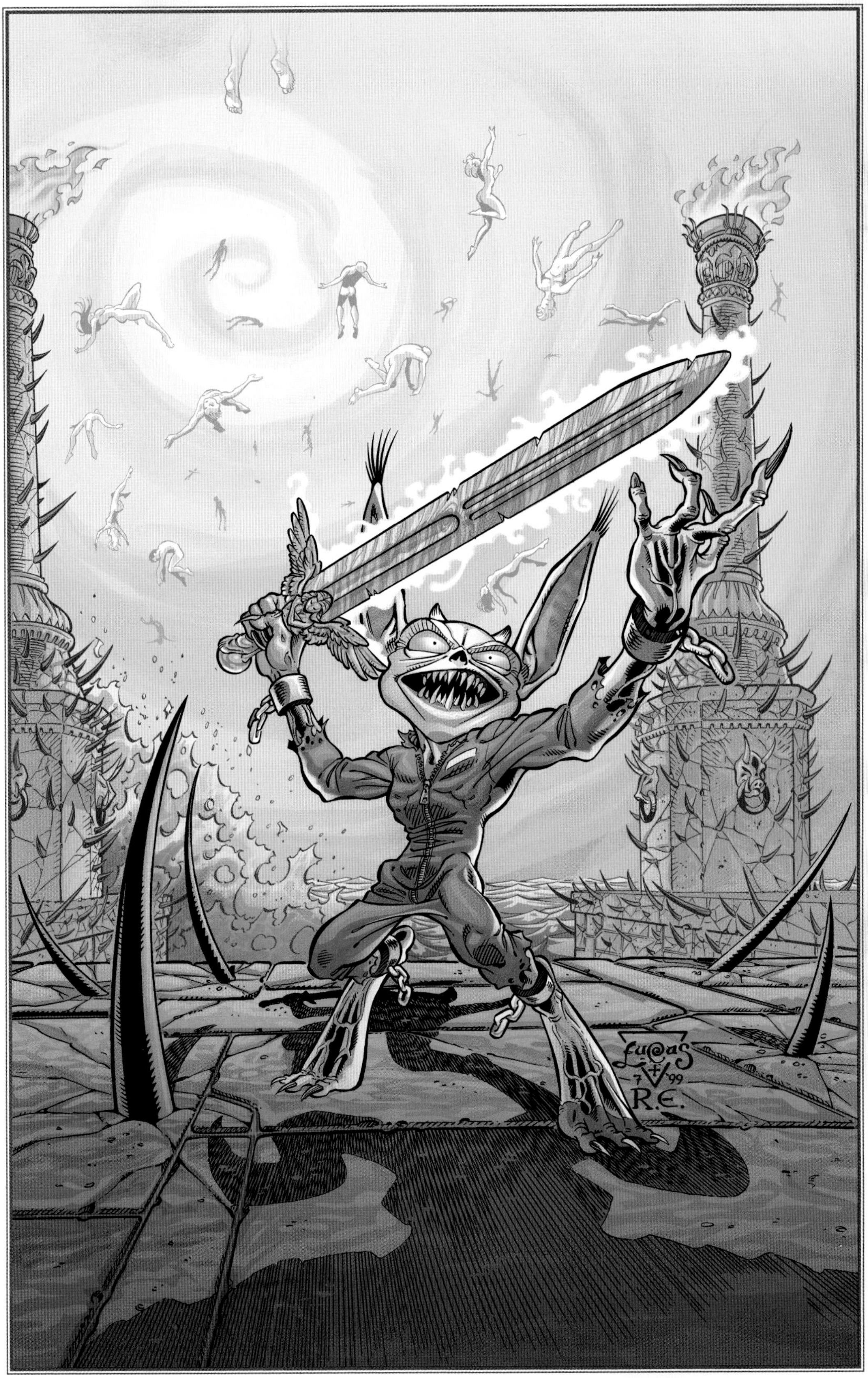
Lucas
7 99
R.E.

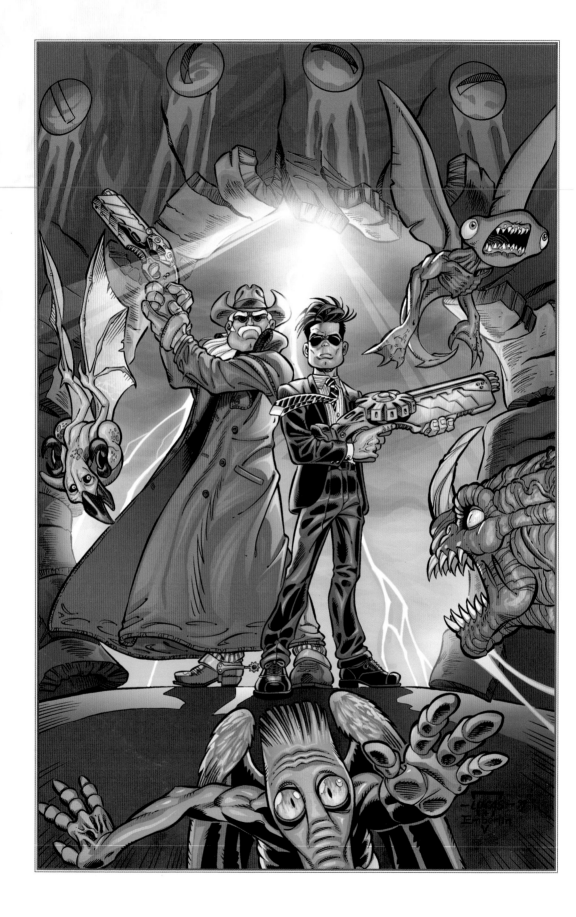